Options

Options

HOW TO DEVELOP AND SHARE
CHRISTIAN FAITH TODAY

Douglas Alan Walrath

THE PILGRIM PRESS
NEW YORK

The biblical quotations marked RSV are from the *Revised Standard
Version of the Bible,* copyright 1946, 1952, and © 1971, 1973 by
the Division of Christian Education, National Council of Churches,
and are used by permission. Other biblical quotations used
have been translated from the original language by the author.

Library of Congress Cataloging-in-Publication Data

Walrath, Douglas Alan, 1933–
    Options: how to develop and share Christian faith today.
    Bibliography: p. 109.
    1. Christian life—1960–   2. Witness bearing
(Christianity)   I. Title.
BV4501.2.W325 1988   248'.5   88-4151
ISBN 0-8298-0779-9 (pbk.)

The Pilgrim Press, 132 West 31 Street, New York, NY 10001

For Sherry,
an honest believer

Contents

Preface

Options fulfills a promise.

In the last chapter of *Frameworks*, the companion book that lays the groundwork for *Options*, I wrote:

> In order to make appropriate suggestions about believing and living to someone, one needs to understand the perspectives through which *that person* approaches believing and living—perspectives that may be quite different from one's own.
>
> The varied frameworks through which people now approach believing and living offer unique challenges to Christians who feel called to share their faith with others. In a subsequent book I plan to describe in detail some approaches that churches can take to meet these challenges.[1]

Options: How to Develop and Share Christian Faith Today is that subsequent book.

In *Options* I suggest some ways those of us who are Christians can develop our own faith and encourage Christian faith in others. I have gained most of the insights I needed to define the options this book suggests by listening to several hundred people describe how they have developed their faith and now share it with others. While I draw on the insights of scripture and faith development theory in order to interpret what I have heard, my primary reliance on the testimony of living Christians makes the book eminently practical.

I acknowledge my debt to all those who have helped *Options* to take shape. I am especially indebted to several people. Over thirty years ago Hugh Baillie MacLean showed me the courage it takes to be an honest believer. I have often been aware of the important foundation he helped me to lay. T. Ralph Morton and David Brown, in widely separated but equally potent conversations, helped me to understand the unique and indispensable nature of Christian discipleship. I am regularly inspired by C. Scott Planting, my pastor. He acts out the faith he talks about—as do others in the small congregation of which I am a member. Together in ministry they nurture my believing, and demonstrate that Christians can live faithfully and significantly today, even in the smallest of churches.

During a conversation I had recently with Robert Lynn, he offered a number of key suggestions that helped to clarify my thinking. On several occasions Truman Fudge has given me the kind of appreciation that helps a writer keep going. And Marion Meyer, my editor at The Pilgrim Press, has again provided just the right combination of critique and encouragement.

Although I certainly do not want to discount the contributions of those I have just mentioned, as I look through the pages of this book, I see again and again how deeply indebted I am to Sherry, my wife. My debt to her is, first of all, personal. During nearly three years, while I have walked about in that preoccupied state that characterizes an author at work, she has given me her constant support. Twice over she has patiently waited for the day when "the book" will be finished.

But Sherry's insights have been as important in the development of this book as her personal support. As I explain more fully in the chapters ahead, she more than anyone else has helped me to understand the difficulties so many people now experience with Christian believing and the church. Sherry grew up outside the church, and for much of her adult life was not a church participant. Yet Sherry came to me and the church full of faith. Her different and difficult road to Christian faith is living evidence to me that God cannot and will not be confined to our standardized approaches to believing. Now that I appreciate her experience I shall never again be tempted to pass off categorically as unbelievers those who are not church participants. Rather, I look for God at work in their believing. And I usually find God at work in their believing. Sherry has both nurtured my faith and widened my perspective.

Douglas Alan Walrath
Strong, Maine

Options

INTRODUCTION

Frameworks and Options

Shortly after my book *Frameworks*[1] was published, I was stopped by a friend who said the book clarified but did not resolve the dilemmas he experiences as a Christian in today's world. He told me of his struggle to maintain an awareness of God's involvement in many areas of his daily life. He described how the church has become less and less helpful to him over the years. "It is much more difficult now to discern how God is involved in the world I live in every day," he said. "Unfortunately I think everything you wrote in that book is true. Your words clarify what I have sensed for some time." Then he asked this probing question: "Now that you have explained what challenges my faith and ministry, what do you have to suggest?"

I responded by saying that I was at work on this book, which I have called *Options*. *Options* is a natural outcome of, in fact, a conclusion to, *Frameworks*. In *Frameworks* I analyzed the social and cultural influences that shape the ways people live and believe today. In the chapters ahead I will describe how those of us who live under these influences can develop Christian faith, and share that faith with others in today's world. The two books are deeply interrelated. Although readers can understand this book without reading *Frameworks*, those who have read *Frameworks* will gain more from *Options*.

In *Frameworks* I describe why so many people struggle today to maintain a Christian theological perspective. The structural "evidence" of God's involvement in daily life, so obvious in a world in which people lived their everyday lives under the shadow of a steeple and the gaze of a pastor, is no longer apparent to most of us. Today we live most of our lives far beyond the reach of either church buildings or pastors. Most adults have never lived in a world in which churches and pastors were able to testify convincingly to God's involvement in their daily lives.

In *Options* I suggest how we can develop and share Christian faith in our world. Most church members who were socialized in times and places in which the church and Christian perspectives were perceived as dominant find the church's current marginal position difficult to accept. As my wife, Sherry, and I consult with churches throughout the United States and Canada we find that most lifelong church members (especially people who are now aged fifty or older) are still surprised to discover that they must *appeal* to younger adults, if they want to attract them to church. And they are even more puzzled (and sometimes angry) when those to whom they appeal do not respond. Yet the evidence is indisputable: many young and middle-aged adults today not only find Christian faith difficult to accept, but also have little sense that they ought to believe it. They do not view Christians as superior. They see other socially acceptable alternatives to joining a Christian church, including not joining any religious group.

Many—perhaps most—adults today do not feel organizationally obligated to take responsible roles in churches; nor are they fearful that some ultimate disaster awaits those who do not become Christians. Although churches that depend

2

on traditional strategies to attract new members or make converts still meet with some success, they are often frustrated. As I consult with congregations throughout the United States and Canada I am repeatedly aware of the little success those who engage in evangelism and church growth have with people who were not Christians to begin with. Most of those who become active in churches or who are counted as converts are actually reactivated church members.

Most of us who are in the church do not understand those who choose not to be part of the church. In fact, we largely misunderstand those we call the "unchurched," and our misunderstanding leads us to relate to them in ways that are neither culturally sound nor theologically justified.

During the early years of my ministry I felt no need to appreciate, much less understand, the unchurched. They were simply an undifferentiated mass of people who did not belong to any church. I felt little need to describe them farther. In my mind, believing and being a church member went together, and so did lack of church membership and lack of believing. If unchurched people were not those who lacked faith, they were at least people with mistaken faith.

Many church members still seem to hold such an organizational perspective on believing. Within such a framework it is easy to assume that the church and God go together organizationally. And that God works organizationally, largely with and through those who belong to (have joined) the church. Our theology is organizationally confined.

By the end of my first decade as a pastor, experiences with both church members and nonmembers had undermined my own organizationally restricted theology. I discovered that nonmembers are no more or no less likely to be lacking or mistaken in matters of faith than members. And I discovered that members often struggle to distinguish how God is involved in their lives and the world at large.

Two seriously flawed implications follow from expecting

God to work organizationally: (1) We assume that those of us who are church members have to take God to those who are not church members; and (2) those of us who are church members do not look seriously for evidence of God's activity in the lives of those who are not church members. In matters of faith we view nonmembers as either empty or misguided. We do not respect their believing.

In reality, almost everyone is likely to have some awareness of God's activity. As the psalmists suggest, awareness of God is a near-universal experience:

> The earth is God's, in all of its fullness,
> the world and everyone who dwells in it   —Psalm 24:1

and

> If I ascend to heaven, thou art there!
>   If I make my bed in hell, thou art there!
>   —Psalm 139:8, RSV

There is nowhere that God is not. The idea that we have to take God anywhere for God to be there is theologically absurd.

So is the idea that God is not involved in someone's life. Scripture makes it quite clear that God is active in the lives of even the most unlikely people. In the Old Testament a non-Jewish king, Cyrus, is termed "Messiah"—a name later given to Jesus. And Jesus himself suggests that prostitutes and tax collectors will probably respond to God's action before even the most respected religious authorities. The thought that we who are church members have to encourage God to become involved in the lives of those who are not church members also is theologically absurd.

But the awareness that many of us have of God is, unfortunately, often vague. Our inability to perceive how God is related to significant aspects of our everyday life is a major issue that faces those of us who are Christian today. So is our frequent inability to help other people develop faith.

Except for a brief period after World War II, when the "renewal" movement occurred, only recently have those of us who compose mainstream churches given significant attention to what is now popularly known as "spiritual formation." Theological education still largely focuses on clarifying what Christians are supposed to believe. Most seminaries do not educate pastors in the art of helping others to believe. Pastors are trained to preach, teach, visit, care, and counsel, but one rarely finds a pastor who knows how to help people develop mature faith. To discover a pastor who sees such equipping as a major aspect of her or his ministry is rarer yet.

My own inability to nurture believing in those who did not grow up in the church came home to me recently in an unexpected manner. Several years ago, Sherry and I met, fell in love, and married. Until we met she had never been an active church member. In fact, except for occasional exposures to the church during her early childhood, she had had no direct contact with the church until we met. As a result, our relationship has provided an unusual opportunity for me to discover what is involved in sharing faith with someone who chose to stand aside from the church during most of her life.

Our sharing has produced two major surprises for me. First, there is no doubt in my mind that Sherry has always had a lively faith. When she thinks about God and describes her experiences with God she often uses images and language that are different from the classic Christian images and language I learned and still use. Yet, as I have listened to her and learned her theological images and vocabulary, there is no doubt in my mind that the God she describes and has always experienced is the same God I know.

The second surprise was the difficulty I found in sharing my faith with my wife. Sometimes it has taken months of conversation for me to understand her perspective on some point of faith, and for her to understand mine. It took us nearly three years to be able to understand each other's way of perceiving God's providence. Only after a great deal of effort did I realize that I can encourage her faith only as I am able to appreciate and use her words. Unless they happen to be meaningful to her, when I use my own words and concepts I am simply telling her what I believe—which sometimes does and sometimes does not nurture her faith.

Reflecting on more than thirty years of ministry in the light of my recent experience with Sherry, I realize how poorly I shared faith with many others during most of those years. To begin with, I thought my major responsibility was to tell others about God—as if they had no experience of God themselves. And although most people to whom I talked listened politely, I now realize that if I had listened to most of them, I would have discovered how poorly I was communicating.

The precondition for nurturing another's faith is respect for the other's believing. When we respect the other's faith as well as our own, we look for God at work in the other's life, and by listening to the other's descriptions seek to help him or her become more aware of God's activity. We listen to discover how the other person perceives God at work in the world, and encourage what seems to us to be authentic in that awareness. When we take a respectful approach to believing, the options we can follow to nurture another's faith become clearer. We discover how we can nurture Christian faith within his or her approach to believing, as well as our own.

Obviously we won't feel called to encourage everything someone else believes. None of us is free from error. Some aspects of another's believing will not seem accurate to us, and if the inaccuracy seems important, we should share what we think. With humility, however! Church membership has never been a guarantee of theological accuracy. Our own approach to faith is not categorically more accurate simply because we are church members.

During the past several years, as I have opened myself more and more to the questions and insights of those with varied approaches to believing, I have found my own faith challenged—and nurtured—as never before. In this book I share the *options* I have discovered.

In chapter 1, I propose an essential attitude that we Christians need to have today. Only as we forgo any claim to inherent superiority will we develop mature faith ourselves and gain the respect we need to have to be able to share Christian faith with others. As I hope I made clear in *Frameworks*, believing in God and living faithfully in today's world are not easy—not even for Christians.

In chapter 2, I suggest that we need to be authentic in both our living and our believing. Many of those who are not within the church can quickly spot any pretense or manipulation on the part of Christians. Indeed, they expect to find both. Before they will want to know anything about our faith, we need to regain the respect of many of those around us.

In chapter 3, I focus on means we can use to nurture our faith to healthy maturity. We will not be helpful to most others if our own believing is confused or immature.

In chapter 4, I suggest ways we can share Christian faith with those around us, and include them in the church. Real options for nurturing others' faith become apparent as we are able to discern how *they* can discover God at work in their living and believing. As we respect the ways in which others approach believing, we discover how to include them in the church—and discover that our own faith is enriched by their believing.

CHAPTER ONE

Forgoing Superiority

A dispute also arose among them, which of them was to be regarded as the greatest. And [Jesus] said to them, "The kings of the Gentiles exercise lordship over them; and those in authority over them are called benefactors. But not so with you; rather let the greatest among you become as the youngest, and the leader as one who serves."

—Luke 22:24–26, RSV

For a long time North American Christians appeared to be superior—in their own eyes as well as in the eyes of others. Now many of us who are North American Christians are discovering that we are not superior. And that to live faithfully as Christians in the contemporary world we need to admit we are not superior. In our own eyes as well as in the eyes of others.

The importance of forgoing any claim to superiority came through clearly to me in 1971. That fall I participated in a conference in Milwaukee, Wisconsin on the contemporary state of Christian missions. The conference organizers hoped that face-to-face communication between church members in my denomination who support mission work and those from mission fields who receive that support would bolster the waning financial support of local congregations for denominational missions. To serve that end they invited leaders of Third World indigenous churches to present their views to several hundred representatives of American congregations. Denominational staff people like myself were asked to serve as facilitators and observers.

Within hours it was clear that the conference would take a direction much different from that anticipated by the designers. The polite and optimistic tone of initial welcoming remarks offered by the hosts were immediately challenged by invited leaders from the indigenous churches.

An Unsettling Confrontation

An African church leader startled the conference participants by suggesting that North American Christian missionaries could help his church most by going home and staying there "for at least a decade." "We Africans need to be out from under your domination," he said. "We can't forge our own identity as Christians with your judging eyes looking over our shoulders. We need the freedom to find ourselves as Christians within our own culture, not as extensions of yours."

Another speaker, a young militant Native American, continued the challenge. "I have a message for those of you who year after year send boxes of clothing to those of us who live on 'the reservation.' Since childhood I have opened those boxes. I don't want to open any more boxes. My people don't want your cast-off clothes anymore. We want our self-respect. Tell your churches not to send us any more cast-offs."

As I listened to conversations around the coffee urn during a break in the proceedings, it was clear that these speakers were having a divisive effect. Middle-aged representatives of North American congregations were shocked and felt uneasy—even outraged—about what they were hearing. Youth and younger adult participants, however, were encouraged by the counterculture perspective of the speakers. Members of the steering committee were worried; the conference seemed out of control. It was.

But as the conference progressed some of us began to appreciate fully for the first time that we now live in a global, pluralistic culture in which North American Christians do not dominate, in which our majority attitudes do not prevail, and in which we are not automatically viewed by others as superior. Not even by other Christians.

In Milwaukee we were confronted by what some of those who are different from us think about us when they are away from us. We heard how they talk about us when they are not under our control. Many of us were surprised and unsettled by what the speakers said.

But after we were able to move past the initial shock, and converse for several days with people from other cultures, we began to see them and ourselves more accurately. Through their eyes we saw that many of the pictures we North American Christians have of ourselves differ from those that others have of us. We realized that some of our attitudes may be more generous and fairer than others think they are; and equally, that some of our attitudes and behavior have been, and are, neither fair nor generous, nor at all appropriate for Christians. We began to see how we have been and still are captive to the prevailing attitudes of our own culture.

As I recall my own unsettling experiences at the 1971 conference, I realize that the trends I saw there continue into the present. Although most contemporary critics are less strident, the scrutiny to which North American Christians are subjected today is even severer than it was in the 1960s. The position of the church in our society is certainly less privileged now than it was then. Right at the outset those of us who are Christian believers, and especially those of us who want to share Christian faith with others, need to know what we are up against.

We need to appreciate the effects of recent social change. Current popular attitudes encourage all of us to view everything and everyone with a most critical eye. As a result, Christians and the church are subjected to more critical scrutiny than ever before. Under such a revealing light our shortcomings are much more apparent. Not even God escapes criticism anymore.

Moreover, critical attitudes formerly held only by those beyond North American society are now prevalent among many within North American society. Although they are less vocal than in the past, many North Americans, especially those within the "baby boom" generation (or "Challengers," as I prefer to call them),[1] still hold countercultural attitudes toward the church.

To some, the observations I have made and now make in the pages of this chapter may seem harsh. But, regretfully, we majority North American Christians are guilty of at least some of the sins to which our accusers point. Where such is the case, we need to face our shortcomings, learn what we can from our critics, and, where appropriate, adapt our behavior. The effective nurture of our own faith and our ability to share faith with others require a candid appraisal of ourselves and the way we now appear. We need to take to heart the ways those who do not reflect our traditional perspectives regard us. Even if doing so means subjecting ourselves to some stiff criticism.

The Debunking of Missions

During the weeks after those days in Milwaukee in 1971 nearly every participant with whom I talked continued to be surprised by what happened at the conference. Even those of us who served as denominational staff, who were familiar with the perspectives of the Third World speakers, had not expected them to confront us so directly. Not within the context of a domestic church gathering.

We went to the conference anticipating a much more controlled flow of information than most of us now take for granted. Although many of us knew better even as early as 1971, we still functioned as if people from other cultures would see us the way we see ourselves—and relate to us accordingly. We still expected them to reinforce our traditional perspectives, especially on our own turf.

Then most of us were still naive middle Americans. We had grown up seeing only carefully selected representatives of other cultures, chosen to match well-defined molds cast by our own culture. As children, those of us who grew up in mainstream churches read about missionaries and natives. Occasionally we saw slides or films about missions. We knew a few missionaries by name. They were held up to us as exemplary Christians, people who gave "full-time, Christian service" (which we mistakenly interpreted to mean they alone were *real* Christians).

Those few "natives" who were displayed to us were also stereotypes. They were chosen to exemplify either the unconverted majority (always poor, diseased, uneducated, and at least seminaked), or the converted minority (always cured, dressed, and civilized). The only individual natives whose names we knew from either reading or direct contact were exceptions: the well-clothed converts. The rest were a blurred mass, seen on the slides shown by returning missionaries and on the pages of *National Geographic*.

When representatives of Native American cultures were brought to our attention either by missionaries or by the media, they were also always stereotyped. They were presented either as good (exceptional) examples or as bad (typical) ones. Thus the Lone Ranger's "faithful" companion, Tonto, was always portrayed as a good (subservient)

Indian, as exceptional; Geronimo was always portrayed as a bad (wild, uncivilized) Indian, as typical. Scores of "cowboy and Indian" movies reinforced our Native American stereotypes as consistently as the missionary slides and *National Geographic* volumes reinforced the African stereotypes.

These caricatures of Native Americans, Asians, and Africans that reinforced our cultural images had a purpose: to motivate us to fulfill our mission obligation. Most of us did so by contributing some money to support missionaries. In those days we truly believed that North American Christian ways were unquestionably superior, and that others would be better off if they adopted them. Thus we were doing natives a favor by converting them. Even if they didn't want or like that conversion, it would still be good for them.

Against such a cultural backdrop it becomes apparent why speakers at the Milwaukee conference startled, frightened, and even angered the majority North American participants. The young Native American seemed more like Geronimo than like Tonto; the African, with his lack of subservience, did not seem quite converted. Neither was properly grateful.

Before the massive social and cultural changes of the 1960s few of us who grew up within the majority, white North American mainstream seriously questioned the cultural stereotypes we inherited. They were present at the beginning of American history, and over the centuries were seldom challenged. In fact, at critical points the myths were reclarified and passed on to each new generation.

In *American Myth, American Reality,* under the heading "Crusade," James Oliver Robertson describes how Europeans who originally settled America brought with them the key elements that would compose our traditional perspectives.

The Europeans envisioned America as yet another place to engage in a Christian crusade. Although political differences might divide Spanish and French and English, and sectarian differences might separate Catholic and Congrega-tionalist and Quaker, they all assumed that Christian civi-lization was superior to all others. They saw Christians alone as fully human, as truly civilized. One could be a heretic and still be a Christian; but even heretics were not classified like the "heathen," as subhuman.[2]

Essential dress and behavior distinguished Christians from those who were not Christians.

Christians wore the proper kind of clothes. Native Amer-icans (like Geronimo) were easily identified as heathen by the way they dressed and fashioned their hair. Those who began to dress like Christians had taken the first step to being accepted as Christian.

Christians settled. They lived in houses and tilled the soil; they did not live in tents and wander. Christians were also identified because they carried out the work appropriate for each sex, and behaved appropriately as men or as women.

Christians attended church services. They did not wor-ship in a mosque or synagogue, and certainly not in a heathen grove.

The mind-set was comprehensive and completely biased. The Christians who came to the New World saw the ways of thinking and behaving that united them as proper and good. They perceived the Native Americans' ways of living and believing as "barbaric," "idolatrous," or "evil."[3]

In his multivolume history of the American people Daniel J. Boorstin shows how these self-perceptions have been reenvisioned in the American mind-set through three cen-turies.[4] We "conquer" the frontier. We "tame" the wilder-ness (and its inhabitants). And then, in the nineteenth century, seeing the subduing of the American wilderness approaching completion, we turn our attention to a similar taming enterprise in other "wildernesses" among other "natives." Even after two hundred years the cultural as-sumptions brought from Europe still come through clearly.

Boorstin shares some representative thoughts from a typical missionary of the time, Cyrus Hamlin, who made his way from a Maine farm through Bangor Theological Seminary to serve as a missionary in Turkey for thirty-five years. Hamlin's perspectives restate the old vision.

> "Almost everything is out of joint," Hamlin observed, in the far-off cultures where the missionary worked. Therefore, he argued, the missionary's secular and religious purposes were inseparable. Where *everything* needed to be "straightened out," only the American Christian missionary could do the job. He brought the gospel of a whole new way of life, aiming not merely to convert individuals but to introduce the "heathen" peoples to the spade and the plow, to the use of bills of exchange, and to "the whole organization of civilized life," in order to hasten the "transition from heathenism to civilization; from utter hopeless indolence to industry; from a beastly life to a Christian manhood."[5]

As the nineteenth century fades into the twentieth, major political leaders, like Theodore Roosevelt and Woodrow Wilson, reenvision our manifest destiny in global terms, and encourage us to act out that global mission in the Spanish-American War and World War I. In the mid-twentieth century the traditional mind-set still engages the American imagination. Both the Rev. Billy Graham and the General-to-become-President, Dwight D. Eisenhower, call their respective evangelistic and military efforts "crusades."[6] They confirm again the way we see others and, just as important, the way we see ourselves.

In a little-known, but important pamphlet Kenneth Scott Latourette, the foremost historian of missions, clarifies that key insight. The North American Christian cultural myth is so significant not only because we try to impress it on others, but also, perhaps even more, *because we tell it so convincingly to ourselves.* Latourette quotes nineteenth-century missionary Samuel J. Mills: "Though you and I are very little beings, we must not rest satisfied till we have made our influence extend to the remotest corner of this ruined world."[7] For a long time many of us believed that, with hardly a doubt.

Throughout our history we majority North American Christians have held a double image. We have pictured the subjects of our missions as inadequate or empty or misguided, even simply as bad. And we have seen ourselves—not just our church, but our culture and our way of life—as full and good, as superior.[8]

What it meant for others to become Christians was equally clear. They had to adopt our faith, our church style, our behaviors, our ways of thinking, even our nomenclature to describe themselves. Some years ago a former missionary told me about his revealing encounter with a woman in India during the 1930s. When he met her on a path he thought she might be Christian. So he asked her about her religion. She replied, "I am an American, Protestant, Dutch Reformed, Indian Christian." Note the order.

Nurtured as we were within such a cultural framework, it is not surprising that the Milwaukee conference was such a jarring experience for most of us North American participants. For centuries our majority cultural perspectives were protected by tacit understandings concerning what we and others should and should not talk about. As long as those who were culturally foreign to us stayed in their places geographically and socially, they weren't present to challenge our cultural myths. We weren't confronted. We saw what we were supposed to see, and wanted to see, and needed to see.

But our heritage is revealed as cultural bias now, a myth more than a reality. The challenge introduced by the "others" at the Milwaukee conference is fundamental. They are spokespeople for a global majority in whose eyes we have lost our superiority.

A Time of Leveling

Looking back I see the Milwaukee conference as a church-related example of the larger social and information revolution that was then transforming our lives. In the late 1960s and early 1970s most of us were still new at coping with the uncontrolled and often confusing flow of information that has now become commonplace.

Perhaps those of us who have lived through both World War II and the Vietnam war can most easily see the contrast. Consider, for example, the difference between the well-controlled information flow during the World War II era and the comparatively uncontrolled flow of information during the Vietnam war. During World War II all the information sources, from the official censors to the moviemakers, cooperated to keep our majority cultural stereotypes intact. Just about all of us accepted the prescribed perspective.

Not so during the Vietnam years. In fact, the greater freedom of information during that era even changed some of our perspectives on the previous era. I recall how startled I was during the late 1960s by some dialogue in the film *In Harm's Way,* which was produced during World War II. The hero, a naval officer, points out the different ways Japanese and American children are raised. American children are given wholesome toys, like trucks and dolls, and taught to be productive and caring. Japanese children are given toy weapons and taught to hate and kill. I was startled because when I had first seen the film, soon after it was released, I had accepted the stereotypes as fact.

Even films made in the years after World War II (like *Strategic Air Command*) were designed to protect our myths. But by the 1960s we were beginning to be able to see another side. I remember watching the movie *MASH,* a film about the Korean War that was made and released during the 1960s. My viewing companion and I laughed openly at the covert manipulations portrayed as commonplace in the film (like taking a jeep and then ordering a sergeant to change the identifying numbers to cover up the theft). On the way home we reminisced about similar incidents during our own experiences with the military.

The new element in the Vietnam era, as compared with the World War II era, was not the manipulations; the new element was the freedom we felt to talk about them. The solemn heroes of World War II films gave way to heroes with foibles. We were seeing and talking about their—and our—foibles. Although many of us knew the truth behind the proverb "No man is a hero to his valet," we pretended that *our* heroes did not have foibles. Now we no longer feel the need to pretend.

Or the possibility of pretending. In his study of the effects of the recent electronic media revolution, *No Sense of Place: The Impact of Electronic Media on Social Behavior,* Joshua Meyrowitz describes the differences between our current information system and a traditional information system.[9]

A traditional information system is marked by an authoritative and well-controlled *pattern* of access to information. Control is in the hands of those who are the appointed guardians of the system. They (like the censors in World War II or the "elders" in traditional cultures) are perceived both by others and by themselves as superior, and therefore capable of deciding what should be transmitted. They decide when and with whom to share what information. The authorities can suppress information or views they think might undermine the prevailing system or culture. They know, and ordinary people believe, that they have the right to exercise control.

Traditional information systems are protected by distance as well as by control. For example, as long as distance prevents most people from seeing all the characteristics of

Africans and Native Americans, or what actually happens in the war zone, they have only the transmitted information or approved examples with which to fashion their pictures of reality. Occasional "untypical" examples who come into view, like the bad evangelist Elmer Gantry or the good Indian Tonto, don't change the accepted impressions of ministers or Native Americans *because they are defined as "exceptions."*[10]

Meyrowitz describes how the proliferation of electronic media in combination with the social revolution of the 1960s has "debunked" the traditionally accepted North American cultural myths for many, if not most, people today. We now are likely to see more than simply what we are "supposed to see." We see more because the flow of information is less controlled and because we believe we have the right to see more. We have a new perspective concerning what we should see.

Meyrowitz uses the analogy of a dinner party to illustrate our new perspective. He describes the traditional difference between "on-stage" behavior, what we are supposed to see, and "off-stage" behavior, what we are not supposed to see. On-stage behavior at a dinner party begins when the guests arrive. Off-stage behavior occurs before the guests arrive and perhaps continues in the kitchen during the dinner party. In a well-controlled setting, whenever the guests are present those who are hosting the party control themselves and the situation to create the impression they want to make.

Our contemporary situation is more akin to a dinner party at which the guests arrive early and discover the hosts embroiled in a heated argument while they are setting the table. The guests see off-stage behavior that they are not supposed to see. As a result, the hosts cannot be as pretentious as they might have been if the guests had not seen this other side of their lives.[11] Especially after repeated experi-

19

ences when they see others engaging in off-stage behavior or are seen doing so themselves, both guests and hosts develop new assumptions about others and themselves.

Most of us now believe there is another side to other people's lives *even when we can't see it;* and if we are astute, we realize that most other people believe there is probably a similar other side to our lives as well. Meyrowitz thinks the electronic media especially have promoted the belief that we ought to view life from a "side-stage" perspective, where we can see both the "on-stage" behavior we are supposed to see and the potentially embarrassing "off-stage" behavior.[12] Television and films have encouraged the belief that we ought to include both perspectives by continually presenting us with both perspectives, within media that give us the sense that we are actually present at what is being portrayed.

Thus, during a television special covering a visit by President Anwar Sadat of Egypt to the White House, President Jimmy Carter, forgetting he is wired with a microphone and on-camera, tells President Sadat that they are about to go into a long meeting and perhaps Sadat might want to go to the bathroom.[13] Of course we know that Presidents, like everyone else, need to go to the bathroom, but we are not accustomed to seeing and hearing them talk about it. At least we weren't in the pre-television era.

Similarly we heard occasional tales of "atrocities" by "our boys" during World War II. But when they came home we assumed that what they did "over there" was off-stage behavior; they seldom talked about it, and the rest of us didn't ask them about it. We regarded them simply as heroes who saved our civilization from the forces of evil. A generation later, however, Vietnam veterans return home to people who *saw* (on television) what at least some of them did, and who in recoil are unable to regard them as unqualified heroes.

When the barriers of space and distance that formerly

protected us from seeing off-stage behaviors break down, heroes fall from their pedestals, and the rest of us lose our innocence. We begin to assume that everyone, no matter how heroic he or she seems, is, to some degree, a pretender who has present or past off-stage behaviors that could compromise whatever he or she appears to be in public. Thus we may still be disappointed, but are no longer surprised, when we learn that a respected political leader is guilty of sexual impropriety, or that a member of the clergy is guilty of sexual immorality and financial mismanagement. We knew they probably weren't really above us to begin with.

A Debunking Generation

Although such a shift in perspectives may seem cynical to some of us, it is not even viewed as radical by those among us who have grown up in a "debunked" world in which it has long seemed normal to "let it all hang out." In fact, many who compose the "Challenger," or early "baby-boom," cohort have long promoted the debunking process.[14]

I remember attending the musical *Hair* and being surprised when the entire cast stood naked on the stage. I asked a younger person what point the nakedness serves in the play. She responded, "Nakedness *is* the point!"

The heroes of the Challenger cohort intentionally reveal the other side of our lives and our institutions. From the perspective of those of us who compose the old, majority culture, the nakedness can be painful. We lose both our superiority and our control.

For example, during the 1960s black North American Christians, descendants of African natives, turn about and confront white North American Christians whose great-grandparents brought Christianity to the African great-grandparents. Black Christians point to white Christians and their church as oppressors of black people. They bring to light the "other side" hidden for generations within traditional white North American churches. And the electronic media display white Christian nakedness for all the world to see. As the young woman said, "Nakedness *is* the point."

Once we lose control over the flow of information, we majority Christians turn out not to be superior—in our own eyes as well as in the eyes of others. After repeated exposures it is difficult to pretend that North Americans are somehow inherently superior, in terms of either religion or culture.

It is much more difficult to pretend that North American soldiers fit the John Wayne/Gary Cooper stereotype. Vietnam veterans have openly shared their horror with all of us, and the media (witness a succession of films culminating in *Platoon* and *Full Metal Jacket*) have offered vivid supporting evidence.

We are now much less likely to suppress evidence that compromises our leaders. We have recently seen both evangelists and candidates for President disgraced by reports detailing their sexual exploits.[15] Only a few years ago we witnessed the first-ever resignation of a President. We now openly discuss the extramarital affairs of former Presidents.

We are now much less likely to believe that ministers and priests live up to the idyllic images presented so consistently for decades in films like *Going My Way*. Contemporary literature reflects the shift in perspective: there is quite a contrast between the heroic pastor portrayed in Catherine Marshall's *A Man Called Peter* and the fallen hero of John Updike's *A Month of Sundays*. North Americans are now as likely to see clergy in terms of the latter as they are of the former. In what may be a reversal of cultural expectations, a recent national opinion poll[16] indicates that many North Americans now have more confidence in military leaders than they do in clergy. More than likely the shift in perspective indicates that ministers have fallen in status rather than that military leaders have risen.

Despite the anxious protestations of an often-vocal minority, who claim that traditional perspectives still dominate, the old sociocultural framework that gave North American Christians a mandate to go forth and convert the world has largely disintegrated. It no longer seems self-evident either to the rest of the world or to most of us that because of some inherent superiority we have as North Americans and/or as Christians, we should impose the way we live or what we believe on anyone.

The Discrediting of Church and God: From Is to Remembrance

I recently asked someone whether she feels guilty when she doesn't attend church services. "No," she responded, "why should I?"

With my traditional upbringing I must confess to a stronger sense of ought about attending worship services. But I have come to the conclusion that such feelings of constraint place me with a minority of Americans today.

The most convincing evidence of that minority status may be the current emphasis of major U.S. denominations. Most are heavily committed to national efforts that fall under the general heading of "church growth." The movement is replete with workshops and literature, and supported by a multitude of how-to manuals, video resources, even computer software. But despite the obvious sincerity of many of its supporters, in many ways current church growth efforts may represent what a Canadian friend calls an "unfortunate case of ecclesiastical nostalgia."

Most of us who are middle-aged and older recall a boom time for the church after World War II. During those years we ministers prayed and our churches enrolled scores of new members. Many of us were quite convinced that the praying and the enrolling were somehow connected. As I have observed in a previous book, by the mid-1960s we were left only with our praying.[17]

Looking back it is easy to see that the post-World War II era was a "seller's market" for the church. Then most people were presold on belonging; the challenge was to convince them to belong to your church. They were already convinced that they should belong to some church. Most knew they would feel guilty if they did not attend worship services, as well as negligent if they did not see to it that their children attended Sunday school. Besides, many were displaced and lonely. In search of jobs, they had been up-rooted (often repeatedly) from traditional communities and neighborhoods in which their families had lived for genera-tions. They were looking for roots, and the church seemed to offer roots. Without realizing what we were doing, we ministers took advantage of people's hunger for roots and their sense that they ought to attend church.

Over the past two decades that ecclesiastical seller's mar-ket has largely evaporated—at least for mainstream denomi-nations. Post-World War II methods of evangelism, updated to incorporate contemporary technology, continue to have some success among those whose mind-set and feelings still reflect the assumptions of traditional North American Christian culture. But in my experience such approaches are seldom effective among those whose lack of these cultural norms moves them to respond "Why should I?" when asked whether they feel guilty about not attending church.

Churchgoing is no longer experienced as a necessity by many, if not most, of those who are now members of social groups that historically have composed the constituency of mainstream American denominations, especially people who are middle-aged and younger. In our consulting work with congregations, Sherry (my wife) and I have seen repeated examples of a cultural reversal. Current middle- and upper-middle-class church participants, especially those who are middle-aged and younger, often tell us that they feel called upon to explain to their friends why they *do* attend church, not why they don't.

As I described in some detail in *Frameworks,* the church is not well regarded anymore by many people who are middle-aged and younger. They still feel that the church let them down, even abused them, during the 1960s and 1970s. To recall the information system theory I discussed earlier in this chapter, they see (and recall) the "other side" of church members and clergy vividly. The church growth movement, with its apparent emphasis on size and results, seems to support their negative images of the church. However well intended and careful the approach, to such people the church growth movement feels more like a recruitment strategy than ministry. To recall the message of a popular song,[18] it appears to be one more example of Christians singing hallelujah while they are trying to sock it to someone.

In the current situation the key issue for many, if not most, people is not deciding what church to belong to. It is discovering or holding on to the belief that God can still effectively relate to most of life. Such a perception is difficult not only for those of us who carry negative feelings about the church; it has become increasingly difficult for most of us.

Perhaps the most telling criticism of the church growth movement is not the most common: the critics' belief that proponents are really most concerned about numbers and results; in other words, that they are more concerned about church survival than about evangelism. In my experience a far greater shortcoming is the unwillingness of so many active church members and leaders, including many proponents of church growth, to appreciate how difficult believing is for many people today.

25

A few months ago my stepson, Bryan, suggested that I read J. Hillis Miller's *The Disappearance of God,* an analysis of five nineteenth-century writers (Thomas De Quincey, Robert Browning, Emily Bronte, Matthew Arnold, and Gerard Manley Hopkins).[19] Nestled within the literature section of the library for more than two decades, Miller's work (like too much of the revealing literature of the past two centuries) has not gained the attention it deserves in church circles. (I am the first person since 1967 to check it out of my seminary library.) The oversight is unfortunate. Miller describes a human condition that seems to be a major theological/spiritual agenda for our time.

> Paralleling the development of urban, technologized life there has been a gradual dissipation of the medieval symbolism of participation. . . . In that old harmony man, society, nature and language mirrored one another, like so many voices in a madrigal or fugue. The idea of the Incarnation was the ultimate basis for this harmony. But it was precisely this belief in the Incarnation which gradually died out of the European consciousness. The Reformation, if not immediately, certainly in its ultimate effects, meant a weakening of belief in the sacrament of communion. Instead of being the literal transubstantiation of bread and wine into the body and blood of Christ, the Eucharist came more and more to be seen in the Zwinglian or Calvinistic manner. To these reformers the bread and wine are mere signs commemorating the historical fact that Christ was once, long ago, present on earth: "This do in remembrance of me." Instead of being a sharing in the immediate presence of Christ, the communion service becomes the expression of an absence.[20]

The shift in emphasis, from "This *is* my Body" (literally) to "Do this *in remembrance* of me" (a symbolic action), has profound implications. These implications may not be readily apparent to those of us who are accustomed to perceiving reality through theological categories. To appreciate the full significance of the shift Miller describes, we need to recognize that he is *not* proceeding theologically, that is, describing what people *should* believe because it is theologically sound for them to believe it. (In some respects Miller is not theologically accurate: for example, his simple lumping of Calvin's and Zwingli's perspectives together, and his assumptions concerning what Calvin actually believed about the eucharist.[21])

Miller is concerned to describe what people *do* experience, not what they should believe. He suggests that God *in common experience* may now be perceived more often as a memory or a symbol than as an actual, available presence. When people approach worship within our current culture, they often perceive God in historical or symbolic terms. In such a situation, Miller affirms, each celebration of the eucharist is likely to reinforce the common perception that God was once actually more present, or experienced as more present, than currently.

Miller describes how the human dilemma that stems from this shift in perspective is reflected in modern literature.

> One great theme of modern literature is the sense of isolation, of alienation, brought about by man's new situation. We are alienated from God; we have alienated ourselves from nature; we are alienated from our fellow men; and, finally, we are alienated from ourselves, the buried life we never seem able to reach. The result is a radical sense of inner nothingness. Most of the great works of nineteenth century literature have at their centers a character who is in doubt about his identity and asks, "How can I find something outside myself which will tell me who I am, and give me a place in society and the universe?"[22]

The shift in perception is radical. Medieval people perceived God everywhere. Their daily lives and liturgical (sacramental) experiences formed an integrated, mutually reinforcing whole. Like the author of Psalm 139, they perceived nowhere that God is not present.

By contrast the most common experiences of daily life for contemporary people are likely to include perceptions of

God's absence.[23] As I sought to demonstrate in my earlier book *Frameworks*,[24] the structure of life in a now segmented world actually discourages a pervasive sense of God's presence for most of us. Our daily experiences now seem to provide evidence of God's absence and impotence.

Why has it taken until the twentieth century for the change in perspective that Miller roots in the Reformation of the sixteenth century to find its way into common experience? Perhaps because until the twentieth century most people still lived their everyday lives in the physical, as well as social, shadow of the church. During these years only a few unusually perceptive people may have felt the full impact of the liturgical shift because clergy continued to be prominent and church buildings still dominated the landscape. The physical proximity of church buildings and the actual presence of clergy in all phases of daily life—government, work, education, social life, and so on—by implication testified to God's presence in all of life.

But that order has now disintegrated, physically and socially. Recent changes in the structure of society have undermined most of the physical "evidence" of God's presence on which we had come to depend. In the urban society in which most of us live we have lost most of the visible evidence of God's involvement once provided by the physical proximity of church and clergy. Today most of our daily living is carried on some distance from church and clergy. The perceptions of daily experience now reinforce the liturgical message that God is only symbolically present, and therefore less potent than in the past.

In fact, in many segments of our lives we may have lost—or failed to develop—our capacity to see the available evidence that could testify to God's presence. In a discussion of William James' concept of "preperception" Rudolf Arnheim points out that most of the time we perceive only what we expect to perceive, and *only in the context[s] in which we expect to perceive it*. The opposite is also true. We don't

28

perceive what we don't think belongs in a given context. We don't even look for it there.[25]

If I apply Arnheim's extension of James' theory to my discussion, the contemporary spiritual dilemma becomes clear. Because we no longer expect to perceive God in many, if not most, of the contexts in which we live, we do not even look for evidence of God's presence in these contexts. Such evidence may be there, but we have lost, or have not developed, our capacity to see it. Little wonder that spiritual formation is emerging as a central agenda in the contemporary church.

Church and culture, liturgy and daily life no longer consist of mutually reinforcing experiences that affirm the presence and reality of God. God, for many of us, is often a "remembrance" more than a presence. Lacking what is commonly perceived evidence, we struggle in many dimensions of our lives to establish what was formerly perceived as self-evident and sacramentally reinforced. And those of us who are preachers discover that our words of encouragement too often fail because those who listen are unable to perceive any confirming evidence. As we admit to what we do not perceive, we North American Christians realize that we are no more superior theologically and spiritually than we are nationally and morally.

But, as I hope to demonstrate in the chapters ahead, with such honesty we are surprisingly better off. We increase the possibilities of faith for ourselves, and we enhance our ability to share faith with others.

CHAPTER TWO

Becoming Authentic

The Mayor put his hand for a moment on Father Quixote's
shoulder, and Father Quixote could feel the electricity of
affection in the touch. It's odd, he thought, as he steered
Rocinante with undue caution round a curve, how sharing a
sense of doubt can bring men together perhaps even more than
sharing a faith. The believer will fight another believer over a
shade of difference; the doubter fights only with himself.
                    —Graham Greene, *Monsignor Quixote*[1]

Despite the rather gloomy picture I painted in chapter 1, I
believe the world today is full of possibilities for Christians.
I want to suggest some ways those of us who are Christians
can develop our own faith and share faith with others. But
before moving on to specific suggestions, I need to address
one preliminary issue: our authenticity as Christians. We
shall not endure as people of faith in today's world if we
pretend to ourselves or to others to be something we are
not.

Struggling with Credibility

Before we attempt to impress others with our faith, we need to tend to our own difficulties with believing. Many of us either no longer know or have not been able to discover how God relates directly to significant aspects of our everyday lives. We cannot envision how God could be involved in some segments of life, and (to recall the discussion of Arnheim's insights at the end of chapter 1) have even stopped looking for evidence of God's involvement in these dimensions of our day-to-day living.

Many of us who are still active in churches became Christians in a time or lived during our formative years in places where the physical presence of church buildings and pastors still testified to the pervasive presence of God. In our formative experience the presence of God seemed widely apparent. We still see and interpret the world of the present through perspectives we formed in the past. These perspectives tell us that certain theological realities (like the involvement of God in all of life) are still true that are not at all apparent to those whose frameworks were shaped in times and places where neither churches nor pastors could be physically present to most of life.[2]

Some of us, in the process of becoming Christians, decided that to be a Christian one must simply assume that Christian perspectives are valid because other Christians hold them. Although we personally may have difficulty seeing evidence of God's involvement in contemporary life, we assume that God must be involved because other Christians say they perceive that involvement. In other words, we assume a vision and integrity on the part of others that we do not have ourselves.

The attitudes within many congregations today actually encourage such a pretentious approach to faith. One common response other Christians offer to those among us who struggle with believing is to encourage us simply to see the world through "eyes of faith." However, in practice, to have eyes of faith may mean denying what seems apparent to our own eyes, or pretending that what is not apparent to us would be apparent to us if we really had faith. In truth, many of us want to have eyes of faith, but we see little evidence of God's involvement in much of life, and we have no idea how to develop the needed faith. In such circumstances faith becomes intellectually heroic or fraudulent: either believing without experiential evidence, or pretending to believe without experiential evidence.

Theological critics are quick to point out that churches and pastors never actually had the ability to demonstrate God's involvement in all of life. I agree. But in the eyes of many Christians they appeared to; now, by contrast, they no longer seem able to witness to God's involvement in much of life. As a result, we must make our way through daily life in a segmented society often without the supporting presence of churches and pastors. Today we are often left to our own devices, and must find a way to believe in contexts that lack the "evidence" available to our forebears. The challenge we face is substantial. How can we believe in God's pervasive presence when there is no evidence? Can we encourage others to believe what is not apparent to us?

In addition to our own struggles with uncertainty, those of us who are church members often find ourselves faced with a credibility gap. My own research among those who are not church participants and/or Christian believers indicates that many of those around us are suspicious of our motives. Given both our history and the current emphasis on "church growth" within mainstream denominations, it is not surprising that many people think our only real concern is to either convert or enlist them.

Many people who are not church members do not perceive church members as primarily wanting to demonstrate and share the good news of God's caring for humankind.

They perceive church members less generously, usually in organizational and/or sectarian terms. They believe that people who accept help from church members sooner or later discover there is a "catch," "another side" (to recall the somewhat cynical perspectives encouraged by the media), even though that other side may not be apparent in their initial contacts with us. In spite of what we say, many people believe our concern is not really to share the benefits of believing with them, but simply to enlist them.[3]

People generally are more critical and suspicious today than they were in the past. We will not stand up well under the critical scrutiny of many around us unless we can demonstrate integrity. Before we seek to impress others with what we believe, we need to test the integrity of our motives and be certain of the authenticity of our faith. In this chapter I want to suggest some ways we can begin to do both.

Earning Respect

In northern New England, where I live, each fall the color of the changing leaves encourages a large influx of tourists. Although many of the locals complain about the increased traffic the tourists bring, the fall "leaf peepers" do represent added income—even to the churches.

Several years ago a friend described what at first appeared to be a typical Saturday scene "on the green" (the park area within the square) in the center of one village. The churches had erected booths to sell their wares: one group was dispensing clam chowder, another barbecued chicken, a third a variety of desserts, a fourth souvenirs. They were all doing what both locals and tourists expect churches to do. Except for one group, members of the smallest church in the village. Instead of advertising desserts or white elephants, their sign read, "Free Clothes for the Poor."

Everyone was surprised. "Are these clothes for sale?"

some of the tourists wondered aloud to those in the booth. "No, we're not selling them," members of the smallest church responded. "We thought that some of you folks from the city who come here to enjoy the fall colors might know people near you who need clothes, and are too poor to buy them. Do you know anyone who could use some of these clothes? We have a variety of sizes, and many articles are new."

Most of the visitors retreated with the embarrassed admission that they didn't know directly anyone who needed clothes, and who couldn't afford to buy them. Occasionally, though, someone did know of a person in need, and was willing to convey the gift.

The reaction of the competing church groups selling their wares on the green was more akin to anger than embarrassment. "Who do you think you are?" and "What are you trying to prove?" were typical questions they asked those at the free clothes booth.

"Oh, we're not trying to *prove* anything," members of the smallest church responded. "We're just trying to act out our faith. If you know of people around here who need some clothes and can't afford to purchase them, please take some of these clothes to them." The response did little to relieve the sense of tension some members of the other churches felt.

By the next Saturday, when the booths were again open for business on the green, the tension had slowly faded. Throughout the day, in increasing numbers, members of other churches contributed clothes to the little church's booth, explaining that they would like to be part of that church's ministry of caring.

Godly people are startling and engaging. In contemporary post-Christian society, especially within the activities of normal everyday life, most of us are surprised to encounter people who are obviously godly. To interact with people who clearly identify themselves as Christians and church members, and who do not try to condemn us, or convert us, or recruit us, or otherwise manipulate us, who simply live out their faith because that is who they are, is equally surprising. Such people are not typical. They startle us.

Like those from the little church, giving away clothes to the poor, the Jesus we encounter in the Gospels also surprises everybody. Interestingly the conditions under which Jesus begins his ministry are surprisingly similar to those we face today. In those times as well only a few unusual people appear to have had any vivid awareness of God's active involvement in daily life. Religious authorities on the whole appear more often as advocates of moral restraint and social control than as enablers of faith. They usually appeal to tradition, seldom to any spiritual experience of their own, in their efforts to gain respect.

Like those encountering the Christians giving away clothes on the village green, people are surprised by what Jesus does, as well as by what he says. "The reality of God is right here at your fingertips," he proclaims (Mark 1:15). And then his actions lend credibility to his words. His words seem authentic, consistent with the way most people experience him.

Jesus speaks *with* authority, not *by* someone else's authority.[4] What Jesus says and does appears to stem from an immediate experience of God. His words and acts are not primarily based on the teachings of others, or on historical evidence of God's activity.

Such immediacy engenders hope in those who encounter him: perhaps God does still touch life here and now. Like the fishers beside the sea, people leave other concerns and go with him. They want to see more.

They do. He enters a synagogue and encounters a "possessed" man. Perhaps because in his insanity this man's purview is not confined only to phenomena accepted as normal by those within his culture, he is free to recognize the active presence of God as he faces Jesus. Through his schizoid personality, a compound of demented and healthy, evil and holy elements, the possessed man blurts out, "What have you to do with us, Jesus of Nazareth? Have you come to destroy us? [Mark 1:24, RSV]" Then, gripped by the presence of Jesus, sensing an unexpected potential, his confusion issues forth in one single recognition: "I know who you are, the Holy One of God [v. 24, RSV]." Jesus responds by commanding the destructive spirit to "Be silent, and come out of him! [v. 25, RSV]" After one last convulsing wrench it does; the man is whole.

The onlookers are amazed. "What is this?" they wonder. Simply "a new teaching"? Hardly; "with authority [literally, 'out of who he is'] he commands even the unclean spirits, and they obey him [Mark 1:27, RSV]." Like those giving away clothes on the village green, Jesus' spiritual potence engenders unexpected hope. God seems present and real. People are startled and engaged.

What happens, in incidents like these, that engenders faith? Let me suggest two key components: First, individuals or a group of people *demonstrate convincingly by word and deed that God is at work in, through, around them.* Their demonstration challenges the limits we have set on our own perception of God. Second, *experiencing or observing their authentic caring, we feel safe with them.* We believe they will not manipulate us. That combination, seeing their integrity and feeling safe with them, encourages us to risk beyond the current limits of our own believing.

Probably we are most able to expand our own faith when we trust the integrity of someone else's faith. We may then be able to permit another's perspective to impinge on our own framework. We want to see and experience what she or he perceives of God. We are drawn into her or his faith.

This summer one of the work groups participating in the housing ministry sponsored by the cluster of small churches where I am a member was assisted by a carpenter hired by a local community action agency. These volunteers from a church in another state spent a week repairing and re-habilitating the houses of rural poor in our county. The agency told the local carpenter that it had sufficient funds to pay him for only two days' work. On the morning of the third day he appeared at the agency and told his supervisor that he intended to work as a volunteer with the work group for the rest of the week. And he did. When the supervisor asked him why, the carpenter responded, "I just want to be with those people. There is something about them that draws me."

The first, essential element that strikes me about Jesus' ministry, as well as the contemporary ministries of those giving away clothes on the village green and refurbishing homes, is its authentic caring. There are no strings attached. Christian caring, whether evidenced by clothes or healing, encourages others to risk beyond the limits of their current faith. To be Christians and to be perceived as Christians today we need to give evidence of authentic caring.

Doubting and Believing

Initially we may find it easier to extend our caring than our faith. When we attempt to widen our believing, we may discover we are handicapped. Even many of us who grew up in the church learned surprisingly little about believing. In fact, much of what we have learned may even hinder our believing.

I have been rereading Sinclair Lewis' novel *Elmer Gantry*. The book traces the story of an unscrupulous evangelist during the early years of this century. Aside from his oppor-tunist nature, as I read his story, I am struck by Elmer's inability to deal with his own doubt—both in public and when he is alone. That inability to face up to what he cannot believe repeatedly misleads him. It encourages him to pre-tend to others, and sometimes even to himself, that he believes what he does not. This pretension, coupled with his need to keep up appearances, undermines his capacity to obtain aid from those who might help him grow in faith.

One of the climactic moments in the novel occurs the night of Elmer's feigned conversion. As he struggles to keep up conflicting appearances to his Christian mother and his agnostic friend, Jim, he is suddenly struck by the thought that he can resolve his dilemma if he can "bring Jim to Jesus."

> Freed from misery by that revelation, he knelt, and suddenly his voice was noisy in confession, while the shouts of the audience, the ejaculations of Judson [an evangelist] and his mother, exalted him to hot self-approval and made it seem splendidly right to yield to the mystic fervor.
> He had little to do with what he said. The willing was not his but the mob's; the phrases were not his but those of the emotional preachers and hysterical worshipers whom he had heard since babyhood.[5]

My experience at the time of my own baptism contains some unfortunate parallels. I was soon to become a teen-ager. In his concern to move us to confess our faith before the dangerous years of adolescence, the pastor of the church my family attended pressed all the members of my Sunday school class to confess faith and be baptized. One by one we capitulated. At the worship service after Sunday school we were presented to the admiring congregation and our parents as candidates. The formal confession and baptism were set for the next Sunday.

During the days that followed I began to question the wisdom of my decision. Finally I shared my doubts with my pastor. He responded with something like, "Oh, don't worry. That happens to everybody. Just go ahead and be baptized. Your doubts will go away."

With such encouragement, and aware of the potential to disappoint my parents and the congregation, I went ahead. But I can still recall the revolting feelings that came over me as I submitted to an act and said words that were not my own.

Also, I discovered that that minister was wrong in his suggestion that my doubts would go away, if I just went ahead. They didn't. He encouraged me into a pattern of deceptive believing, which I maintained because I thought I would stand out at least as abnormal, and perhaps as bad, if I owned up to my questions. I learned to pretend to believe. Only years later, as a pastor, did I discover how widespread pretending to believe is among Christians—and how damaging.

As long as we think it is bad to doubt, we are encouraged to pretend to believe when we don't or can't. That minister, however well intentioned he may have been, misguided me. Help comes more often when we own up to the limits of our faith.

A father once asked Jesus to heal his sick child. Apparently an epileptic, afflicted with convulsive seizures, the child is so sick that Jesus' disciples are unable to help him. In despair the father brings the child to Jesus, describes long years of struggle, and ends with the plea, "If you can do anything, have pity on us and help us [Mark 9:22, RSV]."

"If you can!" Jesus replies, "All things are possible to one who believes [v. 23, RSV]."

But the father's belief has been stretched to its limits, and he pleads for help to move beyond them: "I believe; help me believe where I am not able to believe! [v. 24]" Then Jesus grasps the child by the hand and heals him.

Our believing is *often* stretched to the breaking point in contemporary society. The effects of rapid social change repeatedly undermine familiar descriptions that once solidly defined the interrelationship of God with all of life. Almost every day we walk through theologically uncharted territory. We are often unable to discern God at work.

Unfortunately few Christian groups have developed the resources to help us cope with our questions. Doubters are still viewed, in a moral context, by many as bad. Doubting is still not widely accepted as a normal occurrence in the life of an honest believer.

Pastors who think they are supposed to function as models of faith are among those Christians who suffer most under the weight of unrealistic expectations. Especially during my years as a synod executive I listened on many occasions to the halting words of another pastor describing how he or she was unable to believe something Christians "are supposed to believe." The crisis of faith was compounded by the pastor's conviction that he or she was untypical and bad. Sadly most had needlessly suffered for years because they were convinced that sharing their difficulty would only make matters worse, not better.

The opposite was the most common outcome: sharing their doubts became for most of these pastors a first step to widening their faith. Two thoughts, given to me by people who helped me at key points during some of my own doubting-to-faith experiences, often struck me during my conversations with those pastors: "Doubt is the seedbed of faith" and "Maturity is the ability to live with ambiguity." I often put them together as "Maturity of faith comes from the ability to live with ambiguity of faith."

During a crisis of belief, faith can emerge as a possibility again when someone helps us to realize that the problem is not God's limited reality, but our own limited perception. We are not bad because we are somehow unable to believe; we are unable. Nor does our unbelief have any material effect on God. God has not gone out of existence because we can no longer perceive God's presence somewhere. Our categories of perception have broken down; the framework we are perceiving through is too narrow. When, like the frantic father in Jesus' story, we share those limits ("help me believe where I am not able to believe") we enable others to help us.

An intentional program of spiritual formation has become

an ongoing necessity for most of us today. In chapter 3, I address this matter in some detail. Here I simply want to establish that doubting is normal, perhaps even essential, for Christians now—a sign of honesty and maturity of faith. To experience doubt in the old, integrated world in which signs of God's presence were woven throughout the fabric of life may have been unusual. But to experience doubt in the segmented world of today, in so many places seemingly cut off from God's presence, may not only be normal, but can also indicate that we are in touch with the world around us. Our doubt is evidence that we are not avoiding the ambiguities of life in order to protect outmoded and inadequate theological perspectives. In this sense, doubting witnesses to the strength of our faith.

When we doubt, we openly confess that we are face to face with the limits of our faith. The stress of that confrontation can encourage us to seek resources that enable us to move beyond the current limits of our faith. It is far healthier to be puzzled than to pretend.

One of the people I admire most in the New Testament is a man who is honestly puzzled: Nicodemus. He comes to see Jesus at the end of the day, when there is time to talk. We have only snatches of their conversation. Even so, Nicodemus' words reveal Jesus' powerful credibility in his eyes: "Rabbi, we know that you are a teacher come from God; for no one can do these signs that you do, unless God is with him [John 3:2, RSV]." Yet Jesus' actions and teachings have thrown Nicodemus' faith into crisis. In response to the challenge he is faced with doubts; again and again he wonders aloud, "How can . . . ?" as he struggles against the limits of his framework. Jesus' responses are so simple, yet hauntingly ambiguous. He draws Nicodemus, and all of us, to believe beyond our frameworks: "The wind blows where it wills, and you hear the sound of it, but you do not know whence it comes or whither it goes; so it is with every one who is born of the Spirit [John 3:8, RSV]."

41

The insights of faith are often not completely clear. But the way of faith is. Then, as now, becoming a person of faith is not a casual experience, something that simply happens to us. Nor are the realities of faith available simply as ideas. They are available as insights and are discovered among people of faith. Faith grows among those who doubt enough to become disciples. Faith becomes real to those who are willing to follow along.

Discipleship: Jesus' Pattern for Nurturing Faith

Recently I led a workshop that focused on ways to help people deepen their faith and learn how to share faith with others. At the close of the first session, a participant, a pastor, told me he was disappointed with my lack of attention to "workable approaches," which he defined as practical organizational and programmatic suggestions. He confronted me directly with: "What I really want to know is: how can I change a congregation bent on survival into a congregation committed to mission?"

I am afraid I disappointed him with my response; I still have no pat answer for his question. As we talked it became clear that he thought he could transform his congregation in the way in which he described by employing suitable organizational and/or programmatic approaches. His assumption, quite common among ministers today, seems to be flawed, for two reasons: first, because he assumes that organizational and programmatic approaches will accomplish the transformation; and second, because he focuses on the congregation as a whole. Such thinking leads him to conclude that transforming a congregation is primarily a methodological matter: analyze the needs, make a plan, gather resources, train leaders, introduce programs, and develop the organizational structures necessary to sustain them.

For a time, during my years as a denominational executive, I also believed that sound organizational/programmatic strategies could equip whole congregations to become communities of faith that are able to reach out in caring ministries to others. But experiences to the contrary soon undermined my confidence in such approaches.

For example, for a number of years I administered a denominational policy that required leaders of new church development congregations to complete a "community analysis" to qualify for funding. To complete the analysis leaders had to compile detailed social and demographic information (concerning age, sex, marital status, ethnic composition, education, employment, etc.) for people in the area around their church and then write a "mission strategy" for reaching them. Authors of the policy assumed that congregational leaders who became aware of the needs of those around them would lead their congregations to reach out to them in ministry. After several years it became apparent to me that most of the time local church leaders were completing the required analysis but were not implementing any outreach. There appeared to be no cause-and-effect relationship between gathering comprehensive information about a community and reaching out in caring ministry to people in that community.

At about the same time another staff person in the same denominational office in which I worked sought to discover how local church evangelism committees help congregations reach out to others. His conclusions were even more discomforting than mine. He discovered that congregations with well-organized evangelism committees were *less* likely to be growing than those that lacked such committees!

Looking back over two decades of work with hundreds of pastors and congregations throughout the United States and Canada, I see no convincing evidence of a positive association between effective church organization, church size, or even expanded church program, and the emergence of Christians marked by dynamic faith and caring ministry.

Sometimes the same church leaders possess well-developed organizational/managerial skills and also know how to help people deepen their faith and move into ministry. But the two are not necessarily related. We are just as likely to find Christians reaching out in ministry and sharing their faith in small churches with little or no program as in large churches with a great deal of program.

The essential processes that help us grow in faith and enable us to reach out and share faith with others are not programmatic or organizational. They are relational. Dynamic Christian faith is nurtured relationally within a pattern of Christian discipline. It normally develops among Christians who live in disciplined relationships with God and other Christians. Jesus invites people out of the crowd, and equips them to live by faith by teaching them how to live as disciples. Today when we refer to Christians as "disciples" we often use the term loosely. We need to see discipleship much more specifically. The Gospels set forth a well-defined pattern of discipleship. If we want to grow in Christian faith ourselves and help contemporary Christians become "disciples," we must understand that pattern and appreciate its implications for our efforts today.

Nearly thirty years ago, along with a group of members from the congregation where I was then the pastor, I visited the now well-known Church of the Saviour in Washington, D.C.[6] During a session of the church's School for Christian Living, the teacher, Dorothy Devers, introduced us to a book about Jesus and his twelve disciples: T. Ralph Morton's *The Twelve Together*.[7]

Morton's book is shaped by his reading of the Gospels in the context of his experiences as a missionary in China and later as a member of the Iona Community. (For a description of the Iona Community see Morton's *The Iona Community Story*.[8]) In *The Twelve Together* Morton suggests that we commonly read the Gospels giving attention only to Jesus' ministry and teaching. We overlook the important role of the disciples in Jesus' ministry. Along with Jesus and the crowds, the Gospel writers describe Jesus' focused ministry with the twelve disciples. Morton believes that *this unique pattern of relationships that marks Jesus' ministry with the twelve is a pattern we still need to take seriously today when we want to become and help others become disciples.* When we overlook that pattern we do not discover what we need to know to be able to equip disciples adequately for a life of faith. We receive the teachings of Jesus, but we do not see how he equipped disciples to live by faith. We do not realize that Jesus intended discipleship to be a way of learning to live by faith, not a status given to a few exceptional people.

What are the key components that mark the relationship of Jesus with disciples? How might that pattern inform our efforts to become and help others become disciples today?

Jesus chose his disciples. As Luke recalls the occasion, "In these days he went out into the hills to pray; and all night he continued in prayer to God. And when it was day, he called his disciples, and chose from them twelve [Luke 6:12–13, RSV]." Or, as Mark remembers it, "And he went up into the hills and called to him those whom he desired; and they came to him [Mark 3:13, RSV]."

We can envision the careful sifting and praying as Jesus decides which ones to invite. We cannot help but wonder, as they did, why he chose those he did? Of course, we have the advantage of hindsight: we know, for example, that as a group they were not marked by exemplary piety or behavior. As a group they were not clearly better than others Jesus might have called. But we can identify some characteristics that set them off, that may help us to discover why Jesus chose them. I will summarize these characteristics here and then describe them in detail later in the chapter.

1. *Jesus invited particular people to become disciples because he sensed they were ready to change.* From the Gospel record it appears that he encountered each of the

twelve at what educators now commonly describe as a "teaching moment." They were ready to give themselves to learning and discovery (although most of the time not without a great deal of support and coaxing).

2. *Those Jesus called were suited for the specific ministry into which Jesus invited them.* He chose them because he thought that at the end of their training period they would be able to carry on that ministry.

3. *Jesus felt that those he chose would fit with him.* He believed he could work with them, and that they could respond to his guidance.

In short, Jesus chose those who were ready to make changes in their lives; whom he could envision in the ministry into which he invited them; and with whom he felt he could work.

The process Jesus followed with the disciples is as important to note as the criteria he used to choose them. *Jesus invited the disciples both "to be with him and to be sent out." The being with and sending out are equal in importance, as well as interdependent.* From our vantage point, because we know the whole of the disciples' story, we have a tendency to move on too quickly to the disciples' activity as apostles. We don't realize that they could be sent as apostles in the end only because they became disciples first.

"Come with me and I will enable you to become . . ." is a key phrase in Jesus' invitation. The disciples were enabled to become what they became primarily *by being with Jesus and one another.*

Jesus' pattern of training disciples resembles what is now called "experiential learning." The disciples learned to live by faith experientially, by being with Jesus. Being with Jesus over a period of months afforded them the necessary opportunities to learn experientially.

Experiential learning usually includes both new ways of perceiving and new ways of functioning. The latter are more difficult to learn. One of the courses Sherry and I teach at Bangor Seminary is a practical course in conflict management. Each new group of students passes through similar stages during the course. During the early weeks the students learn *about* conflict management. They learn about various approaches to managing conflict, and can describe how they would use each when confronted by a variety of conflict situations. They are even enthusiastic when we suggest staging a conflict so they can use what they have learned.

Invariably, however, once they are embroiled in actual conflict the students falter. In the midst of a real conflict students fall back into the old patterns they have always used to survive. They understand new approaches but do not yet have faith in them. Faced with this unanticipated discovery, sometimes they become angry at themselves, and at us. One or two may even ask to drop the course! They have learned to think about new approaches, but they have not developed new patterns of living.

Most of those who continue in the conflict management course reap the benefits of their experiential learning. With repeated practice they gain faith in their ability to manage conflict in new ways. Eventually they no longer doubt their ability to manage conflict.

People are most likely to both discover faith and overcome doubt experientially. To make the discovery usually requires time and discipline. Jesus trains his disciples by bringing them into what they first experience as an unfamiliar pattern: a way of living that counts on the presence and activity of God. They experience the ambiguity and doubt that usually precedes growth in faith. Like students learning to manage conflict, Jesus' disciples are often confused and complain, are full of questions and doubts, and wonder if they will ever be able to do what they see. But after some months they begin to be able to function differently. During these months Jesus brings them into his own daily living. They join in his ministry of proclaiming and caring. At the feeding of the five thousand they distribute the food. He shares his vision of God with them, as on the Mount of Transfiguration. He teaches them to pray, and they watch him pray. They learn by trial—and error. And it takes longer than they expect it to take. But in the end they learn to live as though God will be present everywhere, and discover that God is present everywhere.

Morton believes we still learn to live as disciples experientially, by living next to someone who helps us perceive and respond to God *within the ordinary activities of our own daily living.* Our own experiential learning as disciples takes place

in the ordinary affairs of our daily life. If we do not learn this at the beginning we will miss our way. And this initial training takes a long time. Like the Twelve we don't always see the point of it. We want to start further along the way, or at least, to rush on quickly to more obvious tasks. We think that if only we had more time or more money, if we were free of our daily worries of making ends meet and of the future of our families, we'd be better disciples. We'd then have peace to pray. We'd have time for religious work. But Jesus spent a long time with His disciples showing them that if they did not continue with Him in the temptations that ordinary life brought they could not continue in His company. Prayer could wait. This could not. And this could not be scamped or hurried. It was a stage that could never be passed through. All that could happen through their initial training was they should accept that this ordinary life was the constant area of their obedience and of their work and rejoice that it was so. Time and money are the only things that are ours to use: and by "money" we mean not simply cash but all the things we use. That's why we're always short of them. "We have no time," "we have no money" are our only excuses. Yet we cannot love anyone, we cannot pray for anyone, without giving them of our time or of our things. Our life is in terms of our use of time and of money.

Our training in discipleship is our training in ordinary life—

in the daily choices and decisions of common life, in all the questions that life brings.[9]

The disciples respond to Jesus' invitation. Under his guidance they repattern their lives and discover how to live by faith. They discover how God is present within their daily experience. They learn how to count on God's resources as they live faithfully day by day. At the end of their training they are able to live by faith within ordinary life. And the quality of their faithful living challenges others to believe as well.

Contemporary Disciples

Several years ago, in quite humble surroundings, I met some contemporary disciples, prepared according to the Gospel pattern Ralph Morton identified. Sherry and I visited a cluster of small Episcopal parishes in northern Vermont. During the visit we were repeatedly impressed by the quality of discipleship we encountered in the lay leaders of the churches.

Over supper we told Father David Brown, then serving as Canon Missioner to the parishes, how deeply we had been impressed by the lay leaders guiding the life and ministries in the parishes. How had they come about? "What processes did the congregations follow to choose these leaders?" I asked.

The biblical basis and simplicity of David's answer surprised me: "I chose them! Isn't that the way Jesus did it?"

"That kind of choosing sounds risky," I said, teasing him.

"Certainly it is, but I'm just trying to follow Jesus' example. I know it's risky, but even he made one poor choice. Judas certainly wasn't suited for the life and ministry Jesus envisioned. If I make the right choice two times out of three, I'll be content!" A sense of humor and humility are necessities in someone who risks inviting others to venture into discipleship.

David went on to spell out his approach: his concern to identify those ready to make changes, the prayerful manner in which he tries to discern each person's gifts, and his concern to encourage each person into a ministry that matches his or her potential. He then described the disciplined relationship he shares with these contemporary disciples. He told of challenging them, of meeting regularly with them for prayer and study and sacrament, of ministering alongside them. He described how he planned to move on when he judged they could continue without him. (He has since left this ministry to begin a similar enabling ministry in another place.)

Helping someone to develop as a disciple is quite different from choosing organizational or program leaders, David emphasized. Those who are recruited as leaders for an organization are asked to fit themselves to the needs of the organization. Their duties and responsibilities are already spelled out. Only when those who recruit church members to serve in program responsibilities are sensitive to the match between the responsibility and the member's gifts does the organizational responsibility serve to encourage the development of the member's gifts.

By contrast, when one invites another into the discipline of discipleship, the primary focus is on identifying and nurturing the gifts of the person being invited. The one who is inviting must be able to envision appropriately what the other might become and then nurture that person to develop his or her gifts. The possibilities of the person, not the needs of the organization or program, are of prime concern.

When Jesus' pattern is followed, the "program" possibilities emerge from the people, rather than by encouraging people to fit into existing programs or organizations. Perhaps that is why there seems to be so little association between the amount of program or organization a congregation has and the number of church members who become disciples. I now see why my colleague discovered that the presence of a well-organized evangelism committee in a congregation does not necessarily encourage church members to become evangelists. The key factor is not the presence of the committee, but whether people are being invited into a ministry that encourages them to express their calling and gifts.

Disciples are challenged to develop their God-given gifts within a disciplined relationship to God and one another. The leader who invites them nurtures their gifts and encourages their ministries, and shows them how to nurture and support one another. Program and organization may be helpful but are not basic. The leader's insight, and the relationship between the leader and the disciples, and among the disciples, are basic.

A Pattern for All Ages:
"Go . . . Make Disciples"

For generations Jesus' Great Commission recorded in Matthew 28:16–20, has been heard by Christians primarily as a mandate to go forth to proclaim the gospel.

> Now the eleven disciples went to Galilee, to the mountain to which Jesus had directed them. And when they saw him they worshiped him; but some doubted. And Jesus came and said to them, "All authority in heaven and on earth has been given to me. Go therefore and make disciples of all nations, baptizing them in the name of the Father and of the Son and of the Holy Spirit, teaching them to observe all that I have commanded you; and lo, I am with you always, to the close of the age." (RSV)

These verses, which have ranked among the most influential in all scripture, have also generally been misinterpreted. Seeing them largely as a mandate to engage in and support missions obscures the primary focus I believe Jesus intended. Some critics do not believe Jesus actually spoke the words attributed to him. However, whether Jesus actually uttered the words or not, Christians in the early church understood them as a reference to a *particular* pattern of discipleship, and believed that *Jesus intended Christians to honor that pattern whenever they sought to "make disciples."*

When, after the resurrection, the eleven remaining disciples heard the phrase, "Go . . . make disciples," the word disciples called to their minds a pattern of living *that they had experienced:* the pattern of discipleship they knew with Jesus over at least several months, and perhaps as long as three years. They didn't have to try to imagine what Jesus meant by discipleship; they had experienced what he meant by discipleship.

Given that experiential base, those early disciples would most likely have envisioned "teaching them to observe all that I have commanded you" as "teach others to live as I taught you to live." They knew firsthand the essential elements necessary to make others into disciples. They honored those elements whenever they invited others to become disciples. We need to follow the same pattern of discipline to help Christians learn to live by faith today.

What are the key elements in Jesus' pattern?

1. *Jesus chose those he felt were ready to take on the challenge of living as disciples.* He sensed they were at a time in their lives when they could invest themselves in becoming disciples. He knew his "congregation" well enough to know who was ready and able to change. And he knew who was likely to respond to his nurture.

2. *Jesus invited his disciples to become accountable members of a "primary" group.* They became accountable to him, to one another, and, finally, to themselves. Their

relationships with him and one another provided them with the support to engage in the honest doubting of self and God that can lead to secure faith. Jesus knew they would not grow sufficiently in faith until they changed the pattern of their living. Until they saw themselves as disciples responsible to one another and to him, they would escape back into the crowd. He knew they would not discover how they could trust God unless they had to trust God. Jesus knew that disciples require primary relationships of support and accountability to stay with their commitment.

3. *Jesus challenged his disciples to specific ministry. The ministry he held before them was suitable for those he invited.* Jesus taught the crowd and cared for suffering people in the crowd, but he pressed disciples immediately into ministry. Every disciple had to act. Those in the crowd could remain passive and anonymous, but not disciples. They were identified with him, and their actions (or lack of action) would reflect on him, and the group as a whole. It was important for them to be authentic.

4. *Jesus' special relationship with the disciples was temporary.* He focuses attention on them only during the period of their preparation. Once they are able to stand on their own and support one another, he moves on. In fact, his moving-on becomes an enabling factor in their development as mature disciples. Discipleship is a means to faith, not a special status.

If we want to learn how to live by faith today, we have to take seriously the pattern of discipline Jesus developed to help people learn to live by faith. If we want to help others learn to live by faith, we need to learn how to provide a similar pattern of discipline.

I use the word similar intentionally. In contemporary experience the elements that compose the pattern Jesus instituted can take a variety of forms. For example, the twelve supported one another in a primary relationship by living together under the same roof. Some contemporary disciples also share a common habitation (as in the Taizé Ecumenical Community in France, for example). But most do not. As Morton observed, we are not simply to attempt a rote mimicking of Jesus' pattern, as though we had to re-create first-century conditions to live as disciples. But to discover and support our life and ministry as Christians today, we will need to honor the four elements in Jesus' pattern.

Few disciples emerge in contemporary churches because congregations today seldom take Jesus' pattern of inviting and training disciples seriously. The pattern of life in most churches today resembles the crowds in the New Testament; congregations rarely include the elements we have identified as the pattern of life that Jesus lived with his disciples. Most church members primarily see themselves as people to be cared for, or as those who support the ministry of others. They refer to their pastor as "the" minister. Most church members view a good minister as one who ministers well to, or in behalf of, the congregation. Although many church members are faithful in their support of the church and its program, few think of themselves as people called to be in ministry, much less as disciples intentionally learning to live by faith. They seldom envision challenging particular church members to discipleship and investing time to nurture them as something that should engage a large proportion of their minister's time and energy.

But then few of us who are pastors follow the pattern of discipling that Jesus demonstrated either. We shape our ministry most often to fit the pattern Jesus used with crowds. We teach and preach and care for people. We even engage personally in sacrificial and prophetic ministries, as Jesus did. Other church members may be moved by our sacrifices and prophetic ministries. When we are sincerely caring, and preach and teach well, a congregation may grow. But with all we do, few disciples emerge. So few disciples emerge because we fail to honor the pattern Jesus defined for enabling others to live by faith. We seldom concentrate on those who are ready to change, and work long enough with them to help them identify and become established in their ministries.

In chapter 3 I describe how pastors and congregations can use the elements in Jesus' pattern to help contemporary Christians develop the faith they need to engage in ministry in today's world. But I am aware that those who seek to introduce such a pattern of discipline into the life of a congregation today may encounter some resistance. In the last few pages of this chapter I want to describe why that resistance usually emerges, and suggest some ways to cope with it.

In my experience, when one introduces a pattern of discipling into the life of a congregation, he or she may encounter uncertainty and misunderstanding in three areas.

First, questions are likely to emerge in relation to the whole notion of "disciples." Are only some church members to be invited to be disciples? Will all existing leaders be required to become disciples? How will the existing (sometimes denominationally mandated) program and organizational structure of the congregation mesh with the New Testament pattern of discipleship? As one pastor put it bluntly to me: "How in the world will I get my church board members to become disciples?"

One who begins a ministry of discipling should *not* assume that all those who currently hold office or program responsibility ought to be encouraged into discipleship. If being a member of a congregation is understood culturally by most church members in terms of being cared for and supporting the ministry of the church, then those who accept program or organizational responsibilities see themselves simply as more active supporters. They seldom envision accepting program or organizational responsibility as discipleship in the way in which Jesus defines discipleship. When pastors talk about organizational responsibilities using the language of discipleship, church members usually interpret their pastor's words organizationally, in terms of structure or program, not biblically, in terms of calling, or relationship to God.

Given this common understanding of holding office in the church, there is no reason to anticipate that those who want to hold office in the church will also feel that they are called to be disciples. Nor should they. Disciples are not defined by the office they hold. Disciples are not functionally special people who have certain unique or different roles only they can fulfill in the church. Disciples do not necessarily have higher status; they do not have more power or control, nor are they necessarily morally or ethically superior.

To become disciples is not to be given a status or role, an office or specialty. We become disciples when we feel called to enter a pattern of disciplined living that equips and enables us to live by faith in the everyday world. Discipleship is a means, not an end.

Only those who seem to be ready should be challenged to enter into a disciplined relationship. Jesus did not exhort everyone, or imply that everyone ought to be a disciple. The criteria for choosing whom to challenge are personal, not organizational. To imply that all those currently in positions of responsibility ought to function as disciples is unfair. Most accepted their positions with a different understanding of what would be asked of them.

The pastor or other leader who invites church members to discipleship needs to be sensitive to the ability of each person to respond. Is this the right time? Is this an appropriate ministry? No one should be challenged to discipleship simply because he or she holds organizational or program responsibility in the church. Each person's calling and ability to respond are the determining factors, not the fact that he or she currently holds an office. To respond to that pastor's blunt question concerning how she might get her church board members to be disciples: Don't encourage them all; concentrate on those who are ready now.

Second, sometimes church leaders wonder what will happen to those whose pastoral needs may not be met when a pastor focuses so much time and attention on a few seeking to be intentional about their discipleship. The issue behind this question usually is not how the needs can be met (because generally there are lay leaders who could provide the needed care), but whether the pastor should be less available.

In response, again I suggest looking closely at the pattern of ministry Jesus followed. Ordained ministers today seek to emulate only some aspects of Jesus' ministry to the unfortunate neglect of others. Based on the way he lived, it seems clear to me that Jesus did *not* feel he always had to be available to respond to pastoral needs. Likely he could have preached to more people and cared for more people than he did had he been constantly available to the crowds. But he chose not to be. In fact, it appears that Jesus chose to spend nearly half his time with disciples.

Jesus protects time to be away from the crowds for his own renewal and to be available to the disciples. Jesus sets aside time to spend with friends (people like Mary and Martha and Lazarus), to pray, and to be with the few he is helping to become disciples. If those of us who are church leaders, especially those of us who are ordained ministers, believe we should emulate Jesus in our own ministry, then we need to be similarly intentional: to protect time for our own renewal and nurture, and to be available to nurture disciples.

Adding such a focus, and reordering one's ministry to

honor it, may result in misunderstanding. In my own pastoral ministry, when I sought to follow Jesus' pattern of leadership and invited those who seemed ready to take Christian discipline seriously to do so, and then set aside time to spend with them, initially my actions led to misunderstanding and criticism. I suspect that adding such an intentional dimension to an existing pattern of ministry will always be misunderstood initially by some church members.

Two developments may help to clear up the misunderstanding. The gifts of some of those being nurtured eventually issue in caring ministries within the congregation. Church members who do not choose to enter the discipling process experience the benefits. Then, as initial disciples begin to function on their own, and the pastor moves on to challenge and support others, it becomes apparent that focused attention to a few is not given out of favoritism, but out of a concern to enable their ministry. But in the first year or two especially, it is important to take time to explain, and to be patient with those who are slow to understand, or who misunderstand.

Finally, those challenged to enter into discipline may not be immediately clear about the nature of their calling; and those not addressed personally may wonder why others have been chosen for what may appear to be a "privileged" relationship. Again, the Gospels are helpful: the disciples repeatedly misunderstood the nature of their discipleship, and so did those close to them. For example, more than once the twelve resisted the simple caring that needed to become the hallmark of their behavior with one another and with all people—evident, for example, in the unwillingness of any among them to be the footwasher (John 13).

Some of those who were close to the disciples thought that their honored position with Jesus meant that they were especially privileged in God's order, as evidenced in the request of the mother of James and John that her sons be accorded privileged seats next to Jesus at the end of time (Matthew 20:20–21).

On the basis of both my observation and my experience, I agree with Morton's suggestion that we who follow Jesus' pattern will probably have to make our way through many of the same dilemmas that confronted Jesus and the twelve.[10] Along the way there are bound to be times when we misunderstand and are misunderstood. We may even wonder whether we have made the right choices in those we have invited to journey with us, or even in deciding to make the journey ourselves. Sometimes we will doubt God and sometimes doubt ourselves. We will make errors in judgment. But then, so did the twelve. And, like them, we need to continue.

It may take considerable effort to develop the elements in Jesus' pattern in contemporary terms. To become disciples today does not mean simply to engage in a play acting of first-century conditions. Although we do need to take seriously the pattern Jesus followed with the twelve, our own versions will probably take on a variety of shapes. But all of them will need to contain the basic elements that Jesus included with the twelve.

Becoming authentic in Christian faith and life today is a radical option. The society and culture within which we now live no longer provide clear paths or social structures that support Christian believing and living. Quite the contrary. The presence and power of God are not generally apparent to most of us, nor are they supported in most areas of our lives. To live as Christians requires a pattern of discipline that enables us to discern the reality and resources of God in our own lives and in the worlds in which we live. How we can develop the elements in such a pattern today is the subject of chapter 3.

CHAPTER THREE

Developing Faith

While they were talking and discussing together, Jesus himself drew near and went with them. But their eyes were kept from recognizing him. . . .

When he was at table with them, he took the bread and blessed, and broke it, and gave it to them. And their eyes were opened and they recognized him.

—Luke 24:15–16, 30–31, RSV

Developing Christian faith is not a casual affair. The reality of God rarely becomes apparent to those who are not actively seeking God. Nor do those who are simply curious develop an active relationship with God.

Jesus challenges us to be followers, not interested onlookers. Fullness of faith develops in those who continue following. One day Jesus told some of those who had begun to have faith in him, "If you continue in my word, you are truly my disciples, and you will know [literally, 'become intimate with'] the truth, and the truth will make you free [John 8:31–32, RSV].'' When we persist as disciples, we discover God's presence in more and more of our own living. And we mature in faith.

A New Perspective: Faith Development

During their supervised field experience, students at Bangor Seminary who are preparing for ministry in rural congregations sometimes meet with medical residents enrolled in Dartmouth Medical School's special residency program in rural practice. The discussion in the combined group is always animated, as seminarians and medical students discover they confront many similar issues in the process of learning to care for those who live in rural areas.[1]

As the discussion progresses, sometimes those who are learning to practice medicine are surprised to discover that seminary students are learning to approach faith developmentally as well as normatively. With their concern for wholistic health care, physicians in the group show a great deal of interest in the suggestion that emotionally healthy people often have healthier and maturer approaches to believing, and that emotionally unhealthy people are more likely to exhibit immature and unhealthy approaches to faith. Most of us are more accustomed to thinking about faith in terms of what we should believe, or what is right to believe. The notion that people develop in their approach to believing, and that they do so following a pattern associated with recognizable stages in human development, is new.

To look at faith developmentally draws on the discipline of psychology of religion; the focus is more on process than on content. From this perspective faith development is related to psychological development; we look at our own and others' faith at various stages of development in order to see how we function as we go about believing.

Some of those who have extensively studied faith development think that we move through describable "stages," or "styles," of believing as we mature.[2] From this perspective, whether our faith is appropriately mature is just as much a matter of how we approach believing as what we believe. Also, psychological disturbances that afflict us affect our believing as well. When an adult who is immature or troubled psychologically approaches believing, the difficulties or disturbances he or she experiences often stem from the way that person goes about believing. Believing can be mature and healthy, and it can be immature and/or unhealthy.

Some years ago when I served as a denominational executive, a friend who is a charismatic helped me to see the value of such an approach to understanding faith. I was telling him about my inability to be helpful to a pastor who was having great difficulty relating to a charismatic member of his congregation. As I described the behavior and thinking of the charismatic church member, my charismatic friend observed: "If someone who is psychologically immature and has an inadequate theology becomes a charismatic, then that person is a psychologically immature charismatic with inadequate theology. Given the energy most charismatics have, such a person is likely to aggravate himself and those around him. I would deal with him the same way I would deal with any other adult who has a childish approach to believing."

The notion of describing someone's belief (including our own) as inadequate or immature is new—yet promising. If we can describe appropriate ways of believing that tend to be associated with various stages in human development, we may be able to discern links between mature believing (process) and mature faith (content). We may discover that the ways people approach believing at various stages of their psychological development encourage or impede their faith development. We may be able to describe transitions that people go through as they grow in faith, and to learn when and how to encourage these transitions. Those farther along may even be able to provide insights that are helpful to those who are at earlier stages. To recall the frame of reference in chapter 2, we may discover that disciples differ from the crowd not only because of what they believe, but also because they approach believing differently.

In my own attempts to clarify the relationship between discipleship and understanding faith developmentally, I find the work of two contemporary teachers and researchers, John Westerhoff and James Fowler, to be most helpful. Each has learned from the other; in fact, their work is most helpful when it is seen as complementary.

On the one hand, Fowler's research and writing, especially his book *Stages of Faith,* attempt to relate theories of psychosocial development to faith development. He focuses on believing, almost to the exclusion of content. Although his serious attempt to be objective gives strength to his work, it also limits its usefulness to those of us who are concerned to describe the specific faith development of Christians.

Westerhoff, on the other hand, does look at faith development from a specifically Christian perspective. He uses Christian frames of reference and describes the process as occurring within the church. Those concerned with a purely "scientific" approach may find his discussion less useful; those of us concerned with discovering how to encourage faith development within the church may find it more useful.

After acknowledging his debt to Fowler, in his book *Will Our Children Have Faith?* Westerhoff goes on to say:

> At this point, I am prepared to suggest that faith (understood as a way of behaving) can, if provided with proper interactive experiences, expand through four distinctive *styles* of faith. Each style of faith to be described is a generalization, and none are meant to be boxes into which persons are placed; neither are they to be used as judgments upon ourselves or others. I have named the first style of faith, *experienced faith;* the second, *affiliative faith;* the third, *searching faith;* and the fourth, *owned faith.*[3]

Westerhoff then describes the association between faith as a way of believing and the way humans function at various ages.[4]

Children, during their preschool and early childhood, tend to function with experienced faith, that is, faith shaped primarily by their responses to the experiences they have with those around them. Experienced faith is molded by the child's observations and interactions with parents and other significant people within his or her primary relationships.

In later childhood or early adolescence the child, sensing that she or he will not always be identified by primary relationships with parents or extended family may "expand" (to use Westerhoff's image) to affirm her or his faith identity by affiliating with a religious community. This belonging faith enables the person to identify with a larger tradition, to say, "I am a _____." Such a person's style of believing is fundamentally shaped by the traditions and functioning of the community of faith (congregation and denomination) with which she or he identifies.[5]

With the movement into adolescence, children enter a period normally marked by challenging and questioning. If their faith development keeps up with their overall development, their approach to believing embraces the same characteristics. Adolescence is an appropriate time for searching and testing accepted beliefs and traditions. The adolescent needs to shape his or her own identity within those traditions. Such doubting and testing and experimenting are essential if the adolescent is to develop mature faith.

If the searching is done well, the person emerges from the time of testing with what is truly his or her own faith. Owned faith is self-examined faith based on well-tested convictions. The word considered is an accurate term to describe a well-developed approach to believing. Owned or considered faith is truly a person's own; it is an approach to believing that enables a person to cultivate and express his or her unique gifts.

Westerhoff believes that expanding from given and affiliative faith to include searching faith and, finally, owned faith is what the church has historically called "conversion." He believes that such mature, considered faith is God's intention for all of us.

Westerhoff describes faith development within a metaphor of expansion; each style of believing expands out of the previous style of believing. From a complementary, psycho-social perspective, Fowler suggests that our approach to believing develops through various stages, associated with stages in human development. He sees these stages hierarchically. A person's ability to function well at each successive stage depends on solid development at earlier stages. Those who do not develop well at earlier stages find it difficult to function well at succeeding stages.

It is important to see these theories of faith development alongside, not in place of, theological perspectives on faith. I don't want to suggest that the developmental approach contradicts the theological perspective that recognizes faith as a gift of God. I *do* believe that we can have faith because God cares enough about us to come into our lives. Yet I believe also that these new theories of faith development offer important insights into the process of developing faith—insights that are especially useful today. As my charismatic friend suggested to me, adults can be mature and healthy in their approaches to believing, and they can be immature, even developmentally impaired, in their approaches to believing.

Westerhoff, in fact, suggests that many adult Christians today are handicapped by "arrested" faith development. "We also need to be aware that few adults have owned faith, and that is why it is difficult to involve many adults in radical [Christian] community and social action. Typically, adults have had their faith arrested in the affiliative style."[6] If Westerhoff's observation of the contemporary church is accurate, and I think it is, three important implications follow.

First, adult church members whose approach to believing is limited to an affiliative style are bound to have difficulty coping with some of the normal demands that face adult believers. For example, many adult believers struggle with rigid and categorical approaches to believing that are more appropriate in ten-year-olds. They have not developed the capacity to stand back from what they believe and view it critically. When confronted with ambiguities of faith and life, they are likely to respond categorically, "You either believe that or you don't!" or "That's not fair!" Like the Pharisees in the New Testament, such people are trapped in legalism.

Second, those whose faith development is arrested in an affiliative style often act out their believing only, or mostly, in terms of belonging. They identify being faithful with being loyal. As such they are loyal "belongers," organizationally and theologically—people who hold fast to their beliefs and commitment to their church no matter what the challenge. Within their framework, to question is to be unfaithful. Such an injunction against doubting, however, limits their capacity to expand, through normal questioning, to a mature, considered faith.

In congregations where affiliative faith is the norm, church members are encouraged to develop their faith up to the point of belonging and no farther. In fact, those who want to proceed with questioning that could lead them to owned faith are often forced to leave the church to do so.[7] Sadly, many churches and pastors may actually be impediments to Christians who seek to develop the mature faith they need to live and minister in contemporary society.

Third, if a majority of adult church members now function within an affiliative approach to faith, it becomes clear why they become so dependent on their pastors. And the dominant style of ministry most pastors follow encourages such dependent believing. As I suggested in chapter 2, most contemporary pastors seem to emulate in their own ministries *only* the approach to ministry that Jesus followed with the crowd. Jesus usually relates to the crowd like a parent; they depend on him to guide them and care for them. They always view him (and God) in the role of a parent. The continued dependency such pastoring supports discourages church members from maturing in faith. They are never challenged to grow up and become disciples.

To help people expand their believing through questioning to mature, considered faith we need to heed the pattern that Jesus follows with his disciples seriously. Jesus' approach with the disciples is designed to encourage mature faith. Jesus challenges disciples to move beyond the belonging style of believing. He encourages their questioning. For example, at one point he asks them, "Who do people say that I am?" Then, more specifically, he asks, "Who do you say that I am?" In the ensuing discussion they reveal a great deal of misunderstanding. Although Jesus rejects the disciples' attempt to force him into their preconceived pattern of ministry, he neither says nor implies that they are wrong to question (Mark 8:27–33). Jesus repeatedly challenges the disciples to expand their believing beyond the rigid categories of given and affiliative faith. He supports them, but also pushes them, as they struggle with doubt and ambiguity.[8] Jesus' faith is distinguished not only by what he believes, but also by the way he goes about believing.

Jesus encourages the disciples to move beyond childish definitions of their relationship with him (and God). He encourages them to relate to him as adults. He calls them his friends and thanks them for supporting him through times of trial (John 15:15, Luke 22:28). He encourages them *not* to give up their individuality to fit into some prescribed pattern of godliness. He suggests that God will be able to incorporate each person's foibles into a ministry that draws out each person's gifts.[9] The pattern of discipleship that Jesus follows encourages disciples to develop owned faith, to become responsible, adult children of God—and they do.

Developing such mature faith has become more urgent for Christians in our time, which may account for the growing attention the work of Westerhoff, Fowler, and others like them is receiving. The geographical, social, and cultural mobility that has radically altered our lives, especially since

World War II, has increasingly made mature faith much more necessary and, at the same time, more difficult to develop and maintain. We have lost many of the clear, social benchmarks that once supported faith development.

When the church informed all aspects of daily life, people had only to embrace available, well-defined patterns of faith. Most people grew up and lived out their lives within a single denomination, often within a single congregation and community. Each person's spirituality was molded by a common religious tradition, often within a single social context.

But the exclusion of the church from many segments of our daily life, which was apparent to some of us by the middle of this century, was established as common experience by the radical social changes that marked the 1960s and 1970s. Many of us who grew to adulthood during these more recent decades hardly experienced church and faith as related to, much less integrated with, our lives. From the beginning we knew the freedom and felt the burden of being on our own religiously. Believing for us is not a common, shared experience. We rarely share our own individual, spiritual experience with others, or find it affirmed by those with whom we live in the workaday world. For many of us religion is not only personal; it is private.

Among those of us fifty years of age and younger who are active in churches, lifelong members of one denomination or one congregation are increasingly rare. Many, if not most, of us who have been active in churches during the past several decades have participated in a variety of churches. Many of us who matured during the 1960s and 1970s left the church altogether, some of us for as long as twenty years. During the years we stood apart from the church some of us actively explored other religions and spiritual disciplines.

Those of us who are mainstream Protestants today can best be described as eclectic Christians in eclectic congregations. We are individually and collectively a composite of elements drawn from the various religious associations, experiences, and times that have shaped us. Perhaps we share so little of our spiritual experiences with one another because we are so different. We hardly know where to begin. We have so little in common.

The presence of such a variety of believers within many congregations today is as much a challenge to the church as the presence of dependent believers whose faith development is arrested in an affiliative style. An arrested, dependent style of believing is certainly not adequate to meet many of the challenges adult Christians face today. But unfortunately neither are many of the approaches people have developed on their own.

Fowler suggests that those who "leave home" emotionally and geographically especially need to forge their own, mature faith.[10] Most of us now do leave home emotionally and geographically when we become adults. We can no longer depend on the props of a Christian culture to support us. In fact, in our segmented society most of us leave home behind emotionally and geographically every day, when we travel to other segments to work or to play. We leave the church behind (as physical presence) as well. To continue believing where the church is not obviously present we need our own developed faith. When so much of our living is carried on beyond the shadow of the church and guiding presence of pastor it is difficult to function as Christians unless we have developed as disciples. We need a mature and disciplined faith because most of the time we live on our own.

Relationships That Encourage Mature Faith

For several years I have taught a course at Bangor Seminary designed to help prospective pastors learn how to encourage faith development in themselves and others. The approach I use with students is similar to the approach I followed as a pastor when I sought to help members of my congregation expand their faith. Except for the fact that they are intent on preparing to be ordained ministers, seminary students are not that different from other church members who want to grow in faith.

I begin the course by asking students to share with one another what they believe and how they have come to believe. For several weeks we concentrate on listening to one another. The ability to listen perceptively to others, to oneself, and to God is essential if one is to grow in faith, and to help others grow in faith. An excellent way to discover how God works in people's lives, and can work in our own lives, is to listen to others talk about their believing.

The immense variety within our student body at Bangor Seminary turns out to be an advantage. There are as many women as men; some are older (including retirees), others middle-aged, and some fresh from college. World War II veterans sit next to Vietnam veterans. Liberal Unitarian Universalists sit in the same circle with conservative Baptists. Some have been nurtured in the structured liturgy of the Mass and Prayerbook; others in the quiet of Quaker worship. Together we represent a cross section of the mainstream North American church.

In the initial class sessions I try to teach students how to engage in what I call "interpretive listening"—with the emphasis on listening. Although they vary widely in background and perspective, in one respect the students tend to be similar: most of them, even those well along in their theological studies, are unskilled in the art of listening. Bangor students are not unique in this respect; in the typical Protestant seminary, students are taught to talk, not to listen—sadly, not even to God. They are tested often on their ability to express themselves, seldom on their ability to describe accurately what someone else expresses.

For background, I recommend only two short readings: Douglas Steere's essay "On Listening to Another" and Carl

Rogers' essay "Toward a Theory of Creativity."[11] By reading Steere's essay I hope students will begin to understand how listening can help them discern God at work in their own lives and the lives of others. Steere suggests that each of us can learn to discern how God speaks to him or her and, by listening to another, to discern how God speaks to that other.

At some points Rogers' approach seems too permissive, but his "client-centered" perspective helps students learn how to set their own concerns aside so they can focus on what someone else is saying. I ask students to give special attention to the last section of Rogers' essay in which he describes "Conditions Fostering Constructive Creativity." In this section Rogers describes how listeners can provide an atmosphere of freedom and safety that encourages open sharing.[12]

Drawing on Rogers' suggestions, I try to describe and act out the difference between descriptive listening and normative listening. I encourage students to practice descriptive listening. When we listen descriptively to someone our primary concern is to discern and understand what he or she is saying. When we listen normatively we are primarily concerned to judge whether what a person is saying is right or wrong. When we listen descriptively we focus on the other. When we listen normatively we focus on our reaction to the other.

Most students discover that they are much better at normative listening than they are at descriptive listening, especially when matters of faith are involved. Few liberal students, for example, have ever listened to conservatives primarily to discern and understand what they believe and why. And vice versa.

I suggest that we agree to some rules of procedure designed to encourage descriptive listening. During sessions when someone is sharing what she or he believes, other class members may not challenge or criticize what that person believes. Our primary goal in this class is to discern how each person perceives God has been and is at work in her or his life. Our interpretive reflections are designed to help that person discover how her or his faith is nurtured.

What I advocate to the class is not to be confused with a cheap "we-all-believe-in-the-same-God" philosophy. At some point when what someone else believes is radically different from what we believe, each of us does have to decide whether what that person believes seems valid. And to say so. But not in the beginning—certainly not initially among adult Christians. The attitude (all too common among clergy) that our first obligation when we listen to another talk about his or her faith is to tell that person immediately whether the beliefs he or she expresses are right or wrong treats the other as a child. If the other accepts the child role, that acceptance may have the unfortunate effect of impeding his or her maturity of faith.

Our first obligation is to hear the other out. Initially we often find the faith experiences of others difficult to understand and appreciate, especially those whose faith experiences differ from our own. We need to give them the opportunity to demonstrate the integrity of their faith. Other Christians grow up in faith when we respect their experience and treat them as responsible. Their faith is stimulated when we listen to them and support them and challenge them to respond to God's bidding as we are able to see God in terms of *their* experience. We challenge them in the midst of their questioning to own the ways God chooses to nurture and develop the unique gifts created in them.

Many students report these weeks of listening as one of the most important learning experiences in their preparation for ministry. The hours are filled with revealing insights. Students are startled by the variety of ways they approach believing, and by the variety of ways they are and have been nurtured. Theological prejudices fall in the face of convincing testimonies to the activity of God from those we formerly thought we had to oppose. Religious pride collapses in the face of someone's inability to be helpful to another facing a faith-shattering experience. But as class members share their faith journeys they are more often surprised by someone's ability to help them see how God was and is present in their lives. During the years I have taught this course, as I have shared my faith journey with successive groups of students, I have found my own faith enriched by their perceptive comments and encouragement.

With respectful listening we can learn to appreciate the ways those who are different from us believe and are nurtured in their believing. During the weeks of sharing we discover how the faith of various members of the group is nurtured in different ways. Some find that their faith grows most often in times of quiet, when they are alone; others realize that their faith grows more often in group settings, through interaction and conversation. Some gain a great deal from formal, corporate worship; others gain little. Some seek the confrontations of social ministry to strengthen their faith; others are more often nurtured in quiet acts of ministry with those who are ill. Some gain a great deal from studying scripture; others are more often moved to faith by watching a sunset, or gazing at the stars on a clear night.

As we listen to one another's faith journeys, we learn how to help others expand their believing to include questioning faith and, as questions are resolved, to expand their owned faith. We find Carl Rogers' suggestions in his essay on creativity especially helpful as we seek to learn how to provide an environment that encourages Christians to question openly. We study Nicodemus (John 3; 7:45–52) as an example of one who risks open questioning and finds his faith expanded through his questioning.

Although I encourage class members to share their faith questions, I also urge them to expand their believing beyond the questioning stage. The perpetual need to challenge to which some Christians are prone is as immobilizing as the confining legalism that besets the faith of others. While teenagers have the luxury of continued questioning, adults need to move beyond the sophomoric approach exhibited by those who challenge simply for the sake of challenging. As I pointed out in chapter 2, mature believing often includes ambiguity. Mature believers trust God when they cannot be certain.

The mark of mature, owned faith is the person's willingness to take responsibility for her or his own believing. As someone identifies what (and who) especially nurtures her or his relationship with God, challenging that person to define a disciplined lifeway that includes those nurturing elements encourages owned faith.

As a pastor, I often suggested to church members that they write a personal faith history and then examine the narrative to discover what nourishes their faith. I then helped each person to identify factors that need to be included in a personal discipline, a program designed specifically to nurture that person's faith. A person with mature faith knows what is required to nurture his or her believing. And provides for it.

A person moves from belonging faith through questioning faith to owned faith as her or his relationship with God becomes more personally defined. A belonging faith style emphasizes God's relationship to a group, such as the nation Israel or, later, the church. In a belonging style of faith the person is largely dependent on the church and its leaders to define, nurture, and guide his or her faith. Independent thinking or questioning is often perceived as dangerous; "the church teaches . . . ;'' is a much safer approach.

Christians with owned faith still value what the church teaches, but each values what he or she experiences in an immediate relationship with God as well. Although they respect the teachings of the church and church leaders, those with owned faith do not feel constrained to accept their guidance in matters of faith. Like Jesus, those with owned faith recognize that church teachings and even the vision of the most perceptive church leaders is limited. Those who cultivate and live out of a mature relationship with God have faith in God's continuing revelation in their own lives, as well as in the lives of others. Like Jesus, sometimes they will find it necessary to challenge the tradition that has shaped them.

The struggle over whether law (interpreted legalistically) or grace should predominate is a major issue between Jesus and the Pharisees. Jesus lives out of an immediate and individual relationship with God that often threatens the legalistic and tradition-centered relationship to God that the Pharisees emphasize. This classic confrontation, acted out in the New Testament between the Pharisees, who primarily lived in a belonging faith style, and Jesus, who challenged them on the basis of his own immediate relationship with God, is often repeated whenever someone discovers an immediate relationship with God that questions the accepted norms of his or her church.

Sometimes the transition from belonging to owned faith *is* frightening. Those of us who make the transition expand from faith guided almost entirely by the norms of the church to faith guided by our own, individual relationship with God as well. Those who function with belonging faith may oppose the expansion to owned faith both for themselves and others because they fear the loss of control. They may also be uncomfortable at the prospect of accepting more responsibility for their own relationships with God.

But the expansion is necessary. Sometimes the overwhelming focus on tradition and group solidarity that marks belonging faith, and that is appropriate for older children, tends to keep adults overly dependent on the church. God appears to be more present to pastors or other church leaders, or to have been more present in the past, than to "ordinary" people in the present time. Jesus' vivid engagement with God in the midst of ordinary life, and his insistence that the disciples relate to God in the midst of their ordinary living, free them from inappropriate dependence on past and present authorities for maintaining their faith. And as we know from the Gospel record, once they are free to relate to God in their own experience, their faith blossoms dramatically.

In thinking about faith development it is important to heed the metaphors that Westerhoff and Fowler use. As our faith emerges we do *not* leave the benefits of previous stages behind. Westerhoff describes faith as expanding like a series of rings. Fowler describes faith development as hierarchical; each stage builds on the previous stages. The previous styles or stages of faith are not lost as one moves from belonging faith through questioning faith to owned faith; they provide a foundation. Owned faith is the unique fullness of faith God created us to experience. It rests on the history and traditions of the people of God. That tradition, the history and the Law, provides a frame of reference that continues to set boundaries for our living and believing. Moving to owned faith does not eliminate those boundaries. As Jesus suggests, "Think not that I have come to abolish the law and the prophets; I have come not to abolish them but to fulfil them [Matt. 5:17, rsv]."

The expansion beyond belonging faith through questioning to owned faith occurs for the disciples as Jesus enlarges their awareness of God's activity in their own experience. The incidents, stories, and actions that compose the Gospels describe how Jesus guides the disciples to perceive God in the ordinary experience of their daily lives. With Jesus they discover that God is as present now, in their own experience, as in the past. Jesus does not seek to discredit the law and the tradition in their minds; he breaks their utter dependence on them to sustain their relationship with God. As their faith matures, the functional center of their relationship with God includes their personal experience, as well as the "congregation" to which they belong.

Today especially each of us needs to take responsibility for her or his own faith development. Developing a clear and secure sense of individual vocation is equally necessary. We live in a world that bombards us daily with demands and opportunities far beyond our ability to respond. As the media bring each of us face to face with so many more needs than we can meet, how does each of us decide where to invest her or his resources? As we move from home to work to community life, each filled with pressing needs for ministry, how can each of us decide where to concentrate?[13] The people who are most helpful are those who encourage each of us to discern how God has been uniquely at work in her or his life and who then challenge each of us to respond accordingly.

Those who try to force us to fit some predetermined model of what they think it means to be a responsible Christian are usually *not* helpful. Not long ago I led a retreat for pastors of small, rural congregations. We spent the time together wrestling with the important issues that face those who invest their lives in such a ministry. Toward the end of the second day a staff member of the retreat center, an earnest peace activist, met with our group for an hour. She shared her ministry and concerns with the group and then went on to suggest that peace ministry was *the* important ministry of our time, that to be responsible Christians we should subordinate all other ministries to engage in a ministry of peacemaking. Although we admired her commitment, we justifiably questioned her assumption that the vocation that engages her, and for which she is well gifted, should engage all of us.

Each Christian has the right to exercise his or her own gifts in ministries that are appropriate to those gifts. Those with the maturity of owned faith know that no ministry is inherently superior to others. They resist those who challenge their vocations inappropriately. When he was a relatively unknown young monk, in the Abbey at Gethsemane in Kentucky, Thomas Merton's profound thinking deeply moved a young visitor. The thought of Merton hidden away seemed intolerable. "Why is a person of your caliber wasting his life away in a place like this?" the visitor inquired. "Because it's my vocation," Merton quietly responded. Mature Christians do not feel compelled to submit to the definitions of others—even dedicated and well-meaning others. When we own our own faith, we also own our own ministry.

Worship and Faith

One day shortly after the resurrection, on a road that led to the village of Emmaus, Jesus met two grieving disciples. In the shadow of Jesus' death they were desperately struggling to hold on to their faith. Jesus asked them to tell him about their struggle. After they did he told them how he saw God working through him in the events they had experienced. But their despair was so deep that it impeded their vision: they failed to recognize him.

Jesus then broke bread with them. As they watched, his hands and gestures suddenly became familiar; they saw him. In that liturgical moment they gained the insight they needed to believe again. Where they had sensed God's absence, they now discerned God's presence. "Did not our hearts burn within us while he talked to us on the road, while he opened to us the scriptures?" They recognized that all along their difficulty stemmed not from God's absence, but from *their* inability to perceive God's presence (Luke 24:13–35).

Sometimes words are not enough to engender faith—even words spoken by God. Sometimes a symbolic act is needed to move us to believe beyond our ability to define.

During my years as a minister on occasion I have sought to portray the connectedness of God to all of life by asking worshipers to bring to the communion table some token to symbolize their daily life. People usually respond by offering some object that symbolizes an important aspect of their living: the carpenter brings a hammer; the student, a book; the homemaker, a wooden spoon; the politician, an ordinance; the parent, a storybook; and so on. I place the tokens—the books and tools and spoons and all—on the communion table, arrayed around the bread and wine of the eucharist. We then share Holy Communion, surrounded by the symbols of our daily lives. And often we find that the symbols give evidence of a connectedness beyond our ability to define.

Worship should never be far from life. We need to perceive the ordinary, not only the extraordinary, as holy. Like Moses, we need to be regularly surprised by the discovery that the common ground on which we stand is holy (Exodus 3:5). The more extraordinary worship is, the less likely we are to emerge with an awareness of God's relationship to our ordinary day-to-day living. Jesus took the common elements that he and his friends had shared over many months, everyday bread and wine, and held them up to symbolize God's pervasive presence. His message: to a person of faith all that is ordinary becomes extraordinary; all that exists can be discovered as holy. "The earth is God's and all of its fullness [Ps. 24:1]."

Each of us has the capacity to increase the ability to perceive God's presence throughout life. We can expand the limits of what William James calls our "preperception"— the notion that we perceive only what we expect to perceive *and* only in the contexts in which we expect to perceive it. If we accept James's theory (which I introduced in chapter 1) as accurate, then our ability to recognize God's involvement in life is restricted by our preperception. If this is so, then if we could expand our preperception theologically, we could increase our ability to recognize God's involvement. We would then realize that we sense God's absence in so much of contemporary life, not because God is actually absent, but because we have been perceptually equipped to perceive God as absent.

In worship that includes experiences like the communion service I just described, we can reform our preperception. Stimulated by the symbols of the liturgy, the preperception of worshipers can expand theologically. They discover the proximity of their ordinary life to God as that proximity is portrayed in the symbols of ordinary life placed next to the elements of the eucharist, which they have already accepted as symbol of God's presence. When they emerge from worship with expanded preperception, they *expect* to sense God's involvement in new contexts—and then they do! They begin to accept as true the vision of God's connectedness to all of life portrayed in the liturgy.

To enable such envisioning, worship needs to combine historical, mystical, and contemporary elements. Most worship in which I participate is excessively historical. The visual and verbal symbols, the words spoken and the objects held before the worshipers, have an overwhelmingly historical content. Although I do believe that we need to gain a sense of the powerful presence of God throughout history, when nearly all the symbols are drawn from times past and from cultures that are not our own, worship gives us a sense that God was more real, and more present, then than now. It may even give us the sense that God is out of place in this culture and time. The worship that is intended to expand our awareness of God's presence actually increases our sense of God's absence.

For example, most of the scriptural images that are carried over into today's liturgies are rural. As such they provide a strong sense of God's involvement in the lives of those who wrote the scripture and in the lives of those whose contemporary experience is similar. But is God as involved in metropolitan life today as God was in rural life then? Theologically speaking we answer, "Of course!" But when week after week only rural and historical images of God's participation are reinforced in the liturgy, the metropolitan worshiper may have great difficulty perceiving the presence of God in contemporary life. He or she then is called on to make unprecedented cosmic leaps of faith to continue believing.

Some years ago, at a retreat for pastors serving suburban congregations, I heard the late Mark Gibbs, a lay person who wrote insightfully about the ministry of the laity in contemporary society, complain about the lack of connection he often experienced between worship and daily life. "Do you ever read the newspaper in the worship service, as you prepare to lead your congregation in prayer?" he asked us. "And I mean the financial section, not just the international and national news," he went on. "So often at worship services, I hear prayers only for the sick and the downtrodden, the mourners and the alcoholics, the old and the weak, the broken and the poor. God knows they need our prayers, but what about the strong? What does the Gospel say to the powerful? How are the bankers and executives, the scientists and labor leaders to see themselves as godly in the midst of their lives if the issues they face are never held up during worship?"

Mystical experiences in worship need a contemporary as well as a historical point of reference. As a child, long before I was permitted to receive the elements at communion services, I was moved by the solemnity of the deacons when they removed the white linen tablecloth that covered the bread and wine. As we softly sang a hymn they carefully folded the tablecloth and the linen napkins that covered the plates of bread.

I felt solemn but I didn't know why; nor did I know how that solemn sense was to be related to the rest of my life. Years later, during a liturgics class in seminary, the teacher described the origin of the solemn custom. Pigeons often roosted inside European churches. A cloth was placed over the communion elements and then removed just before they were to be served, not for any "holy" reason, but to protect them from pigeon droppings. My mystical feelings, stimulated by the solemn behavior of the deacons during my childhood, never expanded my awareness of God's presence because they had no spiritual root. Such misguided devotion, which lacks the potential of revealing God's presence in contemporary experience, has the unfortunate effect of misdirecting the worshipers' attention and wasting their energy. The worshipers may feel spiritual, but they gain little else.

The overall purpose of Christian worship is to illustrate the sacramental nature of all of life. The worshiper should emerge with the sense that there is nowhere that God is not present. "If I ascend to heaven, thou art there! / If I make my bed in Sheol [hell], thou art there! [Ps. 139:8, RSV] is the reality that worship should convey. The key to encouraging such an awareness is liturgy that represents God over and within all, that testifies visually and verbally to the Providential connectedness that is often so difficult for most of us to perceive in contemporary life.

Louis Dupres suggests that "genuine religion in the present . . . differs from the past in that it integrates from *within* rather than from without."[14] The presence of God in all of life, symbolized structurally in an integrated society by the overshadowing presence of church and the pervasive presence of the pastor in all segments of life, now must be established perceptually in worship. In contemporary segmented society much of our living now occurs in places physically separate from church building and pastor. The structural testimony to God's presence has largely disappeared. Unless the connectedness of God to life is fixed in our preperception by worship, we are not likely to perceive it when we are not at worship. Those who plan worship need to shape the liturgy so that it brings historical, mystical, and contemporary testimonies to God's presence together before us.

To realize that faith has been frustrated at some point in our lives, not by God's withdrawal or limited presence, but by our own limited ability to perceive God's presence, is a key discovery. We now have reason to believe that the cause for lack of faith *anywhere* in our lives is likely to be perceptual, not actual—within us, not beyond us. The grip of doubt on our lives is broken. We know that with God's help we can develop faith. Like the man hungering for Jesus' help to overcome his doubting, we can truly say, "I believe; help me believe where I am not able to believe," and have faith that our plea will be answered.

CHAPTER FOUR

Sharing Faith

When the day of Pentecost had come, they were all together in one place. And suddenly a sound came from heaven like the rush of a mighty wind, and it filled all the house where they were sitting. . . . And they were all filled with the Holy Spirit and began to speak in other tongues, as the Spirit gave them utterance.

Now there were dwelling in Jerusalem Jews, devout people from every nation under heaven. And at this sound the multitude came together, and they were bewildered, because each one heard them speaking in his [or her] own language. And they were amazed and wondered, saying, "Are not all these who are speaking Galileans? And how is it that we hear, each of us in his [or her] own native language?"

—Acts 2:1–2, 4–8, RSV

Therefore let us leave the elementary doctrine of Christ and go on to maturity.

—Hebrews 6:1a, RSV

One day several winters ago when I came home from work a friend—I'll call him Bryan—described an annoying encounter he had had that day with one of our neighbors.

During the afternoon the neighbor had come to Bryan's door. Recognizing the man as a neighbor, Bryan welcomed him into the house but soon regretted the courtesy. The neighbor told Bryan that he had recently become a Christian and had joined a local independent Bible church. "And," Bryan said, "it quickly became apparent that he was out to convert me!

"He battered me with a torrent of words, an endless stream designed to convince me I had to become a Christian, and to warn me about the horrible fate that awaits those who do not. I tried several times to tell him about my beliefs, but he refused to recognize any statement of faith as valid that differed from the precise words and phrases he used. Each time I tried to describe what I believe or to question anything he said, he simply talked louder. I finally just told him to leave. Frankly, I liked him better before he became a Christian."

Faith Development and Evangelism

Some say of people like the Christian neighbor who visited Bryan, "He's gone too far!" Perhaps they would be more accurate if they said, "He hasn't gone far enough."

As Bryan and I talked about his encounter with our neighbor, I could see how frustrated he was with the neighbor's unwillingness to listen to him. And, as Bryan and I reflected on Bryan's experience with our neighbor, it seemed to both of us that the neighbor's faith development is arrested in a rigid, given-faith style of believing. His style of believing shapes his approach to evangelism.

As with most of us, the neighbor's approach to evangelism emerges out of his style of believing. His way of believing, however, is very confining. Because he believes that legitimate faith *must be* similar to his own way of believing, he is unwilling to examine approaches to believing that differ from his own. He does not listen to those with different approaches to believing to discover how they may experience God at work in their lives. By definition, they need to be converted. His sole purpose in interacting with them is to bring them around to his way of believing. Those with this kind of approach to evangelism continue to act out the attitude of superiority that has, unfortunately, so often marked Western Christians (as noted in chapter 1).

Our neighbor will no doubt "win" some converts among those who are vulnerable to his approach. But Bryan will not be among them. Bryan is one of the millions who have separated themselves from the church, and who continue to stand aside from the church precisely because of the attitudes exhibited by Christians like our neighbor. People like Bryan have left the church because those they have encountered in the church are not able to help them grow in faith.

Trapped in an attitude of superiority, our neighbor is able to offer very little that might nurture Bryan's faith. He knows little about Bryan's believing because he is unwilling to listen to Bryan. If he did listen to Bryan, he would discover that Bryan's faith is quite well developed. Although the words and phrases he uses to describe what he believes are not always conventional, he has a lively faith. As I write these words I recall one evening in particular when I listened for two hours as he described the similarities he sees between biblical descriptions of God's presence in the world and contemporary understandings of the universe. I said little during those two hours—a word here and there to affirm or, occasionally, to challenge. I learned much that evening that enriched my own faith. Bryan has a solid, questioning faith. Over the years I have known him I have seen his faith steadily mature. I see no need to attempt to control his believing. God is obviously at work in his life.

In recent years, as I have listened to people like Bryan describe how other Christians have or have not been able to help them with their own faith development, I have become more and more aware of the relationship between faith development and evangelism. When those of us who are Christians engage in evangelism our efforts and attitudes are shaped fundamentally by our own approach to believing.

• If our approach to believing is rigid, out of a given-faith style, we will try to convert others, to convince them to adopt our beliefs and our ways of acting them out.

• If our approach to believing is centered on belonging, we will try to recruit others to become members for our church.

• If our approach focuses on questioning, we will try to draw others into our questioning.

• If our approach is shaped by our own considered faith, we will try to discern how God is at work in and around the others' lives, and to help them recognize and relate to God as they are able.

The securer we are in our own faith, the less need we have to focus on ourselves, and the more able we are to focus on what God may be doing in the lives of others and how they might perceive God. Immature faith limits our ability to be effective evangelists. Styles of believing that are appropriate and helpful as we go through the stages of growing up become more and more confining if we continue to function within them as adults.

The literal tenets of given faith are helpful to young children who have little ability to conceptualize God, but they confine and stifle the faith development of adults.

A belonging style of faith is helpful to older children who are seeking to clarify their identity as believers by joining a church, but it can foster excessive dependency in adults who feel they must depend on a church (and its leaders) to guide them in all or most matters of faith.

A questioning style of believing is necessary to enable adolescents to go beyond the confines of the families and communities that have nurtured them as children. They need interactions with various kinds of believers in order to explore fully how they will relate and respond to God in their own lives. But maintaining a questioning style of believing into adulthood can hold someone in a pattern of rebelliousness that blocks him or her from accepting the real ambiguities of faith, and from moving on to develop a faith that is truly his or her own.

As I indicated in chapter 3, owned faith emerges as an adult clarifies what responding to God means specifically in his or her own life. Adults with owned faith have learned what particular relationships and contexts nurture their faith and strengthen them to live faithfully. They have learned how and where they are called to live godly lives.

I do *not* mean to imply that a mature believer leaves her or his roots behind. Mature faith is nourished by the believer's entire faith development. I agree with Westerhoff's suggestion that our faith expands like a series of rings as it develops. What we are is based on what we have been. The faith of a mature adult still rests on certain givens, is nurtured by her or his association with a faith community, and is challenged by important questions.

As a Christian I believe that there are certain fundamental "givens," like God's life-protecting Law, stated preeminently in the ten commandments. I believe our salvation, and that of the entire creation, rests on the redemptive activity of God, visible in the person and work of Jesus Christ. I believe I am called to belong to and take a responsible place as a member of the church. I also believe that there are certain realities of life that I shall not ever fully understand, like the largely unexplainable presence of evil in a creation ruled by God. My own faith, defined in terms of my own calling, includes certain basic beliefs and questions that I find I share with most Christians.

I realize, however, that not all the givens of my faith are recognized as givens by all other Christians. For example, I believe that God's Law condemns all killing of human beings under any circumstances, for whatever reason. The idea that capital punishment is somehow moral is totally incomprehensible to me. The commandment seems clear: "You shall not kill." No extenuating circumstances or exceptions permitted.

As incomprehensible as it seems to me, I know that many Christians hold other perspectives on capital punishment— as they do on other elements of faith that I accept as givens. The owned faith of every mature believer does not rest on the same givens as mine, is not dependent only on the same kind of faith community (or its leader) as mine, nor consistently undermined by the same questions as mine. The givens, affiliations, and questions on which our individual believing rests vary. We accept different givens, are nurtured by different affiliations, and struggle with different ambiguities.

When we realize the great variety that marks our individual approaches to believing, we recognize that we first need to appreciate another's believing before we can appropriately nurture his or her faith. Before we can *meaningfully* share faith with someone else, we need to discover what givens *that person* holds to and why, how and why *that person* feels (or does not feel) called to belong to a church, what questions *that person* is seeking to resolve, and what particular insights of faith *that person* solidly owns.

An adult who seeks to share faith with other adults but who thinks all legitimate believers must accept only the givens he or she accepts, or must belong to a church like his or her own, or must struggle through the same nagging questions will seek to confine all others to his or her own limited believing. Such a person will seek to convert them, to recruit them, or to engage them in questioning like his or her own. The self-centered believing of such a person will impede his or her ability to respect, and thus to nurture, the faith of others.

Those who must control the believing of others find it difficult to encourage another's faith. To encourage another's believing we need to listen to the way she or he experiences God. We need to learn how to help the other discern God's reality within her or his experience, not how to convince the other to adopt our way of believing. We need to widen our own believing to recognize that God may work in the other's life in ways that are different from those with which we are personally familiar. We need to be inspired by God through the other's experience as well as our own.

Caring: A Foundation for Sharing Faith

Most people interpret others' feelings in terms of their own feelings. At least initially they usually expect others to respond with feelings similar to their own in similar circumstances. That common phenomenon may explain why those of us who are church participants assume that those who are not active in a church feel like they ought to be active in a church, and therefore will eventually participate in church. On occasions when we are absent from church services, we feel as though we ought to be attending. So we assume that most other people probably feel the same.

The opposite is just as likely to be true. Most of those with whom I talk who do not participate in a church do *not* feel guilty about their lack of church participation. They feel like Bryan, who walked away from the frustrating encounter with our neighbor feeling that the church member had the problem, not him.

A second common misconception that those who are active in the church hold concerning those who are not active is their belief that people who stand aside from the church will someday come back because they will discover that they need the church. Although it is true that some nonparticipants turn to the church, especially to a pastor, in times of crisis, most pastors will readily testify that all but a few of these drop away once the crisis is past. Church members can no longer assume that either an emergent need or a nagging sense of guilt will draw many, even most, of those who are not church members into church participation.

Nor are church members any longer automatically afforded respect because they participate in a church. As I suggested in chapter 1, neither Christians nor church members are necessarily perceived as superior by most people anymore. Today church participants are not even assumed to be believers; church participation, having faith, and being an ethical person are not necessarily seen as connected anymore. To describe the church to which we belong or what we believe no longer convinces most people that our faith is worth investigating.

In contemporary society we are more likely to gain the credibility we need to share faith with someone by caring for that person than by holding up our beliefs or our affiliation. Like genuine listening, authentic caring offered to someone builds a bridge for sharing faith with that person. It opens us to another person and another person to us. In a relationship built on caring we can discover how to share faith with someone.

Several years ago at the annual meeting of a researchers' organization to which I belong I was asked to lead a workshop on methods that church leaders can follow to analyze community change. When I arrived to begin the workshop there was only one person in the room. Before long it became apparent to both of us that no one else would attend.

While we waited for others to arrive Peter, the sole participant, and I became engaged in conversation. At first we talked about our work as researchers and church planners. But as I became acquainted with Peter, something else beyond his ability as a researcher impressed me: his faith—especially the way he talked about sharing it with others. So when he suggested that, because he was the only participant, I might want to cancel the workshop, I offered an alternate plan. I proposed that we learn from each other during the remaining two hours. During the first hour I would share my methods of analyzing communities; during the second hour he would describe his ways of sharing faith. Fortunately Peter agreed; he taught me a great deal about sharing faith.

The heart of Peter's approach centers in concentrated caring for a few people for whom he and his wife feel called to care. He described one household in particular, headed by a woman who is a single parent, whom he and his wife have befriended. Peter told me about the dilemmas the woman faced as she struggled to hold a full-time job while carrying all the parenting responsibilities for her adolescent son. Peter was seeking to relieve some of her burden by inviting the son to go with him on occasional outings. Peter described the emotional support he and his wife were offering to the woman as she worked to overcome her bitter feelings toward her former husband. Peter said she also had begun to realize how she contributed to the breakup of her marriage, and that she was working on these issues in a therapy group composed of divorced people. Peter described difficult hours he and his wife had invested trying to help the woman deal with her anger toward God, anger that was blocking her ability to accept God's caring. He told of upholding the woman and her son in prayer.

Peter and his wife have read a number of resources that describe the issues single parents and their children face. They want to be informed in their caring, to be certain the way they care is helpful to those for whom they care.

"It may be some time before we can share our faith overtly with her," Peter concluded. "She has been hurt. People like her need time to recover before most of them can accept anyone's statement that God cares about them. They have to experience a good bit of human caring first."

Respect and response to others' human needs like Peter

and his wife offered to the divorced woman and her son can lead to openings for sharing faith. As I explain more fully in the next section, when we respect and care for someone's human needs, that person is more likely to believe we will also respect and care for her or his way of believing.

There are two key elements in relationships like the one which Peter and his wife have formed with the single parent and her son that make them relationships of respectful caring that can lead to openings for sharing faith.

1. Those who initiate the relationships are concerned to be genuinely helpful. To be genuinely helpful is to care for someone in ways that can be identified as helpful from the other's perspective as well as our own.

At a conference some years ago, when I described how I believe caring can form a basis for sharing faith, a participant challenged me with the following illustration. "Suppose you are caring for an alcoholic," he said. "The alcoholic says he will believe you really care about him if you give him money to buy liquor. Do you give him the money because he says that will show him you really care?"

"No, I wouldn't," I responded. "While he might look upon my money as evidence of caring, I do not believe I am really being helpful to him by giving it. I would not give him money to buy liquor because I do not believe that helping him to continue in what I see as a destructive pattern is really caring for him. It might seem like caring from his viewpoint, but doesn't seem like it is from mine."

But our caring also needs to be helpful from the other's perspective. We do need to take seriously the views of the one we are caring for. Caring that seems to be helpful from our own perspective can turn out to be damaging when we look at it from the other's perspective.

I remember well the insights a divorced woman shared with me while I was working with leaders of a city congregation who were planning a ministry to singles. I had just asked her whether she knew of other churches that were carrying on ministries to singles in that city, and if she did, how she would evaluate them.

"I certainly do," she responded. "The _____ church has a large singles group, and their program has done a great deal of damage!"

"Why?" I asked, surprised by the depth of feeling in her statement.

"The people who run that program seem to think that marriage is the only normal state for adults," she went on. "They think that divorced people are more likely to live together without being married, a relationship that people from that church consider immoral. So their program is designed to encourage divorced people to find someone to marry as quickly as they can. Their program is like a marriage mill. Aside from their bias against people who choose to remain single, the people running the program don't appreciate how damaging a quick remarriage can be. Someone who goes through divorce is usually very lonely during the first few months after the marriage dissolves. But 'solving' that loneliness with remarriage before one has had an opportunity to discover what he or she did to contribute to the failure of the previous marriage can simply lead to another divorce. In the new marriage the person tends to repeat the destructive patterns he or she followed in the previous marriage.

"Someone who divorces needs to identify what he or she did that contributed to the breakup of the previous marriage, as well as have an opportunity to decide whether marriage is a viable option for him or her. While the people in that church think their program is helping divorced persons, from my viewpoint they are hurting at least as many people as they are helping."

When we extend caring that is genuinely helpful it must be genuinely helpful from the other person's perspective as well as our own. When we are deciding how to care we need to respect the other, and evaluate what we are doing from her or his perspective as well as our own.

2. The mature faith of those who begin these caring relationships is a second key element that needs to be present to enable relationships like that initiated by Peter and his wife to lead to openings for sharing faith. The quality of Peter's faith is apparent in his caring. He does not make his continued caring for others contingent on their dealing with his own believing; that would be manipulative. But when those for whom he cares respond to his caring, he is prepared to share faith with them. He not only cares about their human needs; he cares about their believing.

A few years ago I was completing a planning consultation with a downtown church located immediately adjacent to an area of high poverty. For nearly two decades the congregation had supported social ministries to those in the neighborhood. "During those years how many people who have been touched by your caring have become members of your church?" I asked. After an embarrassed silence one of the church members responded, "None."

As we talked together the reason for such a complete lack of response emerged. The church *supports* ministries of caring; the members do not *directly* engage in the caring. Their contributions support a day-care center, a clothing store that offers inexpensive clothes, a soup kitchen that provides meals at no cost or for a nominal charge. But they are not personally involved in the caring as people of faith. Those who receive the care are helped, but they are not directly touched by people they can identify as giving the care *as an extension of their faith*. Although they know the care they receive is supported by a church, they are not directly touched by the faith of those who support that care.

Contrast the caring ministry offered by the group of small congregations I mentioned in chapter 2, who express their concern for the less privileged people in the county in which

I live by helping them to build more adequate housing, or to rebuild homes destroyed by fire. As church volunteers work side by side with those whose houses they are helping to build, there is little in the way of overt talk about believing. Yet, as they work with them day after day, the volunteers are touched by the human needs of those with whom they work. And as they care for these needs, the volunteers' faith sometimes becomes evident to those they touch. Some of those who have received the caring of these volunteers have found their way to Christian believing, and are now members of the congregations offering ministry. They now work alongside those who formerly cared for them, offering ministry to others.

Caring can provide a foundation for sharing Christian faith when those who offer the caring do so as an expression of their Christian faith. Believing that stands behind and that is shared through caring is authentic. And such authenticity is engaging.

How to Share Christian Faith Today

Those among us who feel we have a clear perception of God's involvement throughout daily life are probably a minority today. As I noted in *Frameworks,* and in the earlier chapters of this book, most people in contemporary society, including many Christians, experience themselves as people moving through a world that provides little consistent or pervasive evidence of God's involvement. In such a world the mere fact of our believing is inspiring.

Not long ago a friend told me how her own Christian believing began with such inspiration. She met someone whose way of living gained her respect. She was attracted both by the integrity of his living—his caring actions for others—and by the integrity of his believing. When she shared her own inability to see how God is involved in

96

today's world, he dealt straightforwardly and honestly with the dilemmas she posed.

"In the beginning I could not share his Christian faith," she said. "Yet it seemed believable because *he* believed it. Everything else about him was authentic. I had gained so much respect for him that I had to respect his believing."

Often the first act of faith that someone can venture is to trust the believing of another. Our believing is much more likely to inspire others to faith than our beliefs are. Our beliefs represent the language we use to describe our believing. As such they are one step away from believing.

The language we use to describe our believing may or may not enable another to describe her or his believing. If we insist that someone use our language before we will recognize that person as a valid believer, we may undermine our ability to encourage faith within that person. We are more likely to help another come to Christian faith when we can describe Christian faith within the other's language, experience, and culture.

Such was the twofold experience of those present on Pentecost, that day when the Holy Spirit burst into human experience (as described in Acts 2). Those present were struck first by the believing of the inspired disciples. They could not explain what they saw within the usual categories of human experience. It was evident that the disciples were being moved by God, not by something mundane—like too much wine. Second, each person heard the disciples' testimony in her or his own language. Each was able to interpret the spiritual experience in terms that made sense to her or to him.

Sharing Christian faith is most often such a two-stage process. We can communicate Christian faith to someone when that person is first inspired by our (or another's) believing, and then when we are able to interpret the inspiration in terms of that person's language of faith.

We need to discover how to connect the inspiration someone experiences to the evidence of God that that person has seen, and perhaps not understood. We need to help that person approach believing within his or her framework—the perspectives through which he or she approaches living and believing.

Although such an eductive approach to sharing faith has always been mandated by the gospel, it is even more essential now. Most people today are not willing to give up their language and culture to become Christians; they will become Christians only when Christian faith makes sense within the language they use, and relates to their own culture.

While a few pioneering missionary-evangelists recognized the importance of defining believing within the language and culture of the one with whom we are seeking to share faith, most of us first acted on that insight in our ministry with minority groups during the 1960s. We realized for the first time that our majority ways of thinking and talking about God, and of acting out our faith, are often not suited to minority cultures.

But during that era the pluralistic nature of even our majority culture became apparent. What we had always experienced as a single culture suddenly became fragmented. With their large numbers the baby-boom generation established themselves as a distinct culture. Unable to use the insights of their forebears to find their way in a world of radical social change, baby-boomers turned to their peers for guidance and self-understanding. Before long they developed their own "in" language, music, mores. A new phenomenon emerged, unprecedented in our experience. Our children distinguished themselves from us. They became a "cohort," a generation who pass through such fundamental experiences that they distinguish themselves as a culture in time, in much the same manner as national or ethnic groups experience themselves as cultures.[1]

We responded with innovative ministry to the unusual

baby-boomers, but most of us underestimated the depth of the change. We mistakenly identified the baby-boomers in our minds as a "youth culture." We responded with stepped-up youth ministries, and later young adult ministries and singles ministries. We learned their language and how to use that language when we worked with them. We even made some adjustments in our overall church life. For example, we adapted our worship and educational approaches to accommodate their freer and more participatory style. Sometimes we supported and even participated in their social action. Some of us even found their ways closer to the mandates of the gospel than the ways of believing and living within which we were nurtured.

But most of us did not understand the baby-boomers as a culture. We understood them developmentally. Although they might delay maturing, sooner or later they would grow up and become adults like us. Mistakenly we thought they would eventually give up their Challenger ways and fit into our culture. They would come around and adopt our ways of living and believing.

Of course, some of them did. But many did not, and have not, and will not. Even those who outwardly conform and "come back" to church are often inwardly still different. As I indicated in *Frameworks,* the baby-boomers, whom I named "Challengers" to identify them more accurately by their challenging attitudes and approaches to living and believing, were shaped *fundamentally* by the experiences of the 1960s. They continue today to approach living and believing through their own unique framework, composed of the attitudes and approaches to living they shaped during their prime time. And the pluralistic nature of our society tells them they have the right to hold on to that framework.

In *Frameworks* I suggested that the same social change that distinguished the Challengers as a cohort has encouraged those of us who preceded them also to distinguish ourselves by the approaches to living and believing we defined in our own prime time: the Great Depression and World War II. Our struggles through those years fashioned us as "Strivers"; and we remain unusually committed to hard work and the institutions we struggled to defend. Like the Challengers, we approach believing through our own self-understanding. It feels right and it works for us.

But when those of us who are Strivers insist that members of the Challenger cohort (or any other group who share a common culture) must "come around," and fit themselves into our more traditional approaches to living and believing, we deny the reality of their culture. And we severely limit our ability to share faith with them.

Only as we are willing to give up claims to cultural superiority and to move beyond the confines of our own culture are we free to identify what I will call "openings"— the places in another's experience where God is speaking, or might speak, to him or her.[2] The key question each of us needs to ask when we seek to encourage faith in another is how God is inviting that person to believe. The clues, the openings, the needed words and experiences are much more likely to appear within the other's culture than our own. To discover those openings we need to learn the language the other uses, and to immerse ourselves in the culture that has shaped her or him.

In *Frameworks* I have described in detail how the three contemporary cohorts that compose mainstream American society today approach living and believing. (The third cohort, composed of people socialized in the mid-1970s and 1980s, I call "Calculators," to emphasize their sober approach to living and believing in a world of shrinking options.) I do not intend to repeat those descriptions in this book. They are already available in *Frameworks*.[3] Here I want to go on to illustrate how those descriptions can help us to discover openings for sharing faith with those who are culturally different from us.

In *Frameworks* I suggested that for Strivers, "God is

taken for granted and seen as essential,'' while for Challengers, "God is defined personally and is optional.'' Then I went on to develop that description:

> God is one of life's givens for Strivers, the core of the American way of life. We are a nation under God. Strivers are good "scouts" who do their duty to God and country. . . .
>
> People who don't believe in God do not seem normal to Strivers. They appear as curiosities, people who, for some reason, do not believe "what we all know is true. . . .
>
> No such harmony and stability mark the religious experience of Challengers. . . .
>
> Charlene's brother, Chuck, struggles to find the personal resources he needs to cope with his war experience. Probably discouraged by his sister's and others' disappointing experience with the church, he doesn't even try to search for those resources within the church. After a long search he finally seeks help from a Zen master. His picture of God and way of believing are clearly of his own making, drawn from a variety of sources.[4]

Charlene and Chuck are characters I made up, but the incidents they relate are similar to those that other members of the cohort they represent have shared with me.

Not long ago I was with a group of people who began talking about their experiences during the Vietnam years. One of them, a person the same age as Chuck, suddenly found himself relating an incident he said he had never shared with anyone. He told about piloting a helicopter gunship, and being ordered to attack a village that was reportedly occupied by enemy soldiers. After the attack was over, when they landed and entered the village, he discovered, to his horror, that it had been occupied only by women and children, all of whom had been killed in the attack, and whose bloody corpses lay before him. As he finished telling about this incident, he said he felt ill, and left the room.

Later, when he felt somewhat better, I took a walk with

him. I listened as he struggled to come to terms with the horrible experience that he had allowed to come back to him. Having done such a terrible deed, how could he ever stand before God? he wondered. How could he even hold his head up as a human being? His guilt was so overwhelming that he was unable to conceive of himself and God together. Since his separation from the service, he said he had become active in the peace movement. He wondered out loud why he had not "had the guts to refuse to go." He berated himself as a total moral failure. Then he became conscious of my silence; he looked at me and asked, "What have you got to say?"

How could I know what to say? I'm a Striver; my cohort fought World War II. The horror was no less. But we were neither theologically nor morally ambiguous about our involvement. Hitler and Tojo personified evil. We had to stop them—whatever the cost. There were mistakes along the way; we killed innocent people. We regretted that; some of us never got ourselves together after the war. But the job had to be done. Had we not opposed the forces of evil they would have overwhelmed us. More than forty years later it still seems that way to most of us. We regretted some of what we did, but we have confessed that and, with a sense of forgiveness, we go on.

Sadly, none of my cultural experience with war suggested an appropriate faith-engendering response I might offer to my younger friend. He experiences his involvement in that later war, not as inevitable, and as ultimately justified. He sees his involvement as the result of his lack of moral backbone. If he had "had the guts to refuse to go," he would not have been a party to killing those helpless women and children. His faith was stymied by that traumatic incident. He recalls it not as an act of necessity, but as a horrible sin.

What to say? I let myself go into his experience. A verse of scripture came to mind: Jesus' words on the cross, "Father, forgive them; for they know not what they do." I shared it. We wept together as he found faith.

For most of those beyond the church to find faith God must be defined personally. The familiar categories that define faith for those of us who have always been Christians either do not work for them, or are not enough for them. Many must question their way to faith. As I suggested in *Frameworks,* the normal approach both Challengers and Calculators take to faith includes questioning.[5]

Sometimes one helps such believers find faith by supporting their questioning, rather than by suggesting answers to their questions. For such people faith is sometimes experienced as the ability to believe while questioning. Last year on the last day of a conference I was leading I met a woman in her thirties who was part of another group beginning a conference on spiritual exploration led by Morton Kelsey. I asked her why she found Morton Kelsey's writing helpful. "Because he has a sense of the mystical," she told me. "He does not feel everything can be defined, or needs to be defined."

The nurturing potential of mystery and awe, often facilitated by those who sit quietly with us, is often underrated by those whose faith was developed primarily in relationships in which someone talked about God. In a revealing article, which appeared recently in *The Christian Century,* Paul G. Johnson described a weekday evening service at Augustana College in Rock Island, Illinois, that nurtures those who are not helped by liturgy filled with talk.

> There was no liturgy or sermon. Instead, with the lights dimmed, students sat in silence until they were individually ready to go to the altar railing to receive communion from the chaplain. The chapel was usually filled, and to the surprise of the more "religious" students, the service seemed to draw students never seen at the regular Sunday worship hour.[6]

Silence may hold more spiritual potential than talk for those who grew up in an age of verbal and intellectual confusion.

Ours is a complex and diverse society, composed of people whose approaches to living and believing reflect the various cultural experiences that have shaped them. Of course, cultures offer clues, not prescriptive suggestions, about the ways people approach believing. Not everyone who is nurtured within a given culture approaches believing in exactly the same way. Some do not approach believing at all in the manner typical for most of those who compose their cohort. Some have rejected their culture and have adopted the patterns of another, or assembled a pattern of their own making. People shift and move about freely in our pluralistic society. Discovering how to nurture the faith of others is very challenging today.

But our ability to share Christian faith with others always begins with our own believing. Often the fact of our believing is sufficient to give another hope that he or she can believe. But to nurture another's believing we must go on to learn that person's language and enter that person's culture. Then we are more likely to be able to help that person discern the openings through which God will come to nurture his or her faith.

Concentrating and Including

With such variety of people around us, how do we decide where and with whom to concentrate our ministry?

Personally, I consider my gifts and sense of calling when I decide where and with whom to concentrate my ministry. There are certain kinds of people with whom I find it easier to share faith. I seem to understand them better, and they seem more often to be helped by my efforts. From time to time there are others who come into my life with whom it is not as easy for me to share faith. Sometimes I discover that God wants me to try to share my faith with the most unlikely people. So I remain open to those who, at first sight, appear as people unlikely to benefit from my ministry. But in my overall ministry I am guided by the gifts I believe God has given to me, and the belief that God calls me to use these gifts to share faith with others.

Similarly, the congregation of which I am a part defines the ministries it can offer on the basis of our common gifts and our corporate sense of calling. As a church, we offer significant ministry to the less fortunate in our area in the form of a housing ministry. But we do not offer any ministry to the 2,000 college students who live in our town. None of us has both the gifts and sense of calling needed to sustain a ministry to them.

Every congregation can best define the ministries of caring and evangelism it can offer by honoring the gifts and callings of its members, especially those who have the clear commitment and discipline required to sustain an intentional ministry. Developing an adequate ministry to those with special needs, or to people who are culturally different from the majority of the members requires a long-term investment. Usually churches can sustain only those ministries in which committed members feel called to invest themselves. It often takes years to develop a ministry that will lead to opportunities to share faith with those who are different from ourselves. We have to learn how to meet their needs in ways that are genuinely helpful to them. Before we can help them appropriately toward faith and faithfulness, we need to understand their culture and to learn the language they use to describe their believing. Finally, we need to incorporate elements that nurture their faith into the program and worship of our church.

I do not mean to imply that a church that extends ministry to a different group should transform its entire church life to meet their needs. In fact (and I expand on this point below), leaders need to be especially sensitive to the needs of existing members whenever the church is initiating a new ministry. However, focusing a church's efforts can be helpful for at least three reasons. First, when leaders concentrate on a new group of people they are usually better able to develop the special skills needed to minister to those who compose that group. Second, the church becomes identified within the community as a congregation especially able to minister to a certain kind of person. Finally, when the concentration of efforts is apparent to the community the congregation is more likely to attract others who want to join in the ministry with which it has become identified.

I have already noted above that the small congregation of which I am a member cooperates with other small churches in a housing ministry. We are known for this ministry. People who need help with their housing come to us, as do those who want to engage in that ministry. The woman I met at the retreat led by Morton Kelsey is a member of a large suburban church that concentrates its efforts on Challengers. That congregation provides unusual help with spiritual formation and offers a range of opportunities to those who feel called to engage in social ministries. Another congregation I recently visited concentrates its outreach on alcoholics. The pastor is a recovering alcoholic, and unusually well equipped to help alcoholics with spiritual formation.

The investment necessary to establish a ministry to those who are different can stress a congregation. In fact, reaching out to those who are different, and especially encouraging them to participate in a congregation before existing church members are prepared to include them can result in severe tension in a congregation. I have described how to cope with stress that may arise as a result of reaching out to and including those who are different in the third chapter of my book *Leading Churches Through Change*.[7] Those beginning to reach out in ministry to people who are different in culture from those who compose the majority of their current congregation will probably find that chapter helpful. Here I offer only some words of caution and some suggestions.

From time to time my wife, Sherry, and I are called on to work with a congregation that has reached out in ministry to new people only to discover that the existing members were unable to accept the new people when they became active in the church. Almost without exception when we visit these conflicted churches we discover that the outreach to new people was carried on only by a handful of members who did not take the time to prepare the congregation before they began it. Often only the minister is the agent of outreach. Also in such situations we usually find that the sympathies of those reaching out are with the new people, not with the existing congregation. Existing church members complain that the minister and other leaders are concentrating entirely on the needs of the new people.

When a pastor and other leaders in a congregation feel called to initiate a ministry to people who are different from most of the members, they need to take time to prepare the congregation. The resources Robert Gribbon has developed to help congregations understand young adults provide a useful model.[8] They consist of both interpretive pamphlets that explain the different ways today's younger adults approach believing and the church, and a six-session program a congregation can follow to acquaint members with these differences. The material provided in these resources shows how to help a congregation understand people who are different, and how to prepare a congregation to include them.

I do not mean to imply that a majority of church members must be willing to engage in a congregation's ministry of outreach to new people. But *some* of the *longstanding* members must be willing to support the outreach, and a majority need to understand it well enough to approve of it. A church's pastor(s) needs to be especially careful to maintain her or his ministry among existing members whenever a congregation initiates a new ministry.

When making changes or adding programs that benefit new people, it is important to affirm those programs that meet the needs of longstanding members as well. If church members gain the impression that whatever serves the needs of new people will be added at the expense of program that serves their needs, they will probably oppose the changes or additions. New programs should be seen as additions, not replacements. When those who engage in ministry to new people take the time to prepare the congregation, they are more likely to find support when they seek to include programs or changes in the congregation's life that will serve the needs of the new people.

When a congregation is prepared to receive them, new people who have discovered vital Christian faith can become a source of enrichment and renewal for the whole church. Those of us who reach out to other people and who struggle to share faith with them often discover that they become the very people who reach back and enrich our own believing.

Notes

Preface

1. Douglas Alan Walrath, *Frameworks: Patterns of Living and Believing Today* (New York: The Pilgrim Press, 1987).

Introduction • Frameworks and Options

1. Douglas Alan Walrath, *Frameworks: Patterns of Living and Believing Today* (New York: The Pilgrim Press, 1987).

Chapter 1 • Forgoing Superiority

1. See my *Frameworks: Patterns of Living and Believing Today* (New York: The Pilgrim Press, 1987), ch. 3.
2. James Oliver Robertson, *American Myth, American Reality* (New York: Hill & Wang, 1980), p. 37.
3. Ibid., pp. 38–39.
4. See especially Daniel J. Boorstin, *The Americans: The Democratic Experience* (New York: Random House, 1973), part 10.
5. Ibid., p. 563. Boorstin quotes Cyrus Hamlin, *Among the Turks* (New York: Robert Carter & Bros., 1878).
6. Dwight D. Eisenhower, *Crusade in Europe* (Garden City, NY: Doubleday, 1948).
7. Kenneth Scott Latourette, *Missions and the American Mind* (Indianapolis: National Foundation Press, 1949), p. 28. See also pp. 31–40. While Latourette makes the point I attribute to him, his tone is understandably more sympathetic than mine in the current context.

8. For a thorough history, see William R. Hutchinson, *Errand to the World: American Protestant Thought and Foreign Missions* (Chicago: University of Chicago Press, 1987), especially the Summary, pp. 203–9.

9. Joshua Meyrowitz, *No Sense of Place: The Impact of Electronic Media on Social Behavior* (New York: Oxford University Press, 1985).

10. For a complete discussion of this phenomenon see Michael Polanyi, *Personal Knowledge* (Chicago: University of Chicago Press, 1958), ch. 9; and Douglas Alan Walrath, *Frameworks: Patterns of Living and Believing Today* (New York: The Pilgrim Press, 1987), ch. 1.

11. Meyrowitz, op. cit., ch. 3. See also Erving Goffman, *The Presentation of the Self in Everyday Life* (New York: Anchor, 1959).

12. Meyrowitz, op. cit., p. 47.

13. Ibid., p. 48.

14. For a complete description of this cohort, see Walrath, op. cit., chs. 3 and 5.

15. Evangelists Jim and Tammy Bakker and Presidential-aspirant Gary Hart during 1987.

16. Conducted during 1987 by the Gallup Organization.

17. Walrath, op. cit., chs. 1 and 2.

18. *Games People Play* by Joe South. Copyright © 1968 by Lowery Music Co., Inc., P.O. Box 9687, Atlanta, GA 30319.

19. J. Hillis Miller, *The Disappearance of God* (Cambridge, MA: Harvard University Press, 1963).

20. Ibid., pp. 5–6.

21. See Thomas M. Lindsay, *A History of the Reformation* (New York: Charles Scribner's Sons, 1925), vol. 2, pp. 52–60.

22. Miller, op. cit., pp. 8–9.

23. See Louis Dupres, "Spiritual Life in a Secular Age," in *Religion and America, Spiritual Life in a Secular Age,* ed. Mary Douglas and Steven Tipton (Boston: Beacon Press, 1982, 1983).

24. See Chs. 2 and 4 in Walrath, op. cit.

25. Rudolf Arnheim, *Visual Thinking* (Berkeley: University of California Press, 1969), ch. 5. See also William James, *The Principles of Psychology* (Cambridge, MA: Harvard University Press, 1981).

Chapter 2 • Becoming Authentic

1. Graham Greene, *Monsignor Quixote* (New York: Washington Square Press, 1983), p. 53.

2. See my *Frameworks: Patterns of Living and Believing Today* (New York: The Pilgrim Press, 1987), chs. 1 and 2 for a full discussion.

3. See Vicki Williams, "Flattery: New Tack in Proselytizing," *Central Maine Morning Sentinel,* Feb. 16, 1987, p. 26.

4. See the exegesis on the phrase *"hos eksousian echon"* as used both in this passage and in Matthew 7:29, *The Expositor's Greek Testament* (Grand Rapids, MI: Wm. B. Eerdmans Publishing Co., 1956), p. 136.

5. Sinclair Lewis, *Elmer Gantry* (New York: Harcourt, Brace, 1927), pp. 47–48.

6. For a description of this congregation see Elizabeth O'Connor, *Call to Commitment* (New York: Harper & Row, 1963).

7. T. Ralph Morton, *The Twelve Together* (Glasgow: The Iona Community, n.d.).

8. T. Ralph Morton, *The Iona Community Story* (Glasgow: The Iona Community, n.d.).

9. Morton, *Twelve Together,* op. cit., pp. 135–36.

10. Ibid., p. 135.

Chapter 3 • Developing Faith

1. See David Hilfiker, *Healing the Wounds: A Physician Looks at His Work* (New York: Pantheon Books, 1985).

2. See James W. Fowler, *Stages of Faith: The Psychology of Human Development and the Quest for Meaning* (San Francisco: Harper & Row, 1981); John H. Westerhoff III, *Will Our Children Have Faith?* (New York: Seabury Press, 1976), p. 89.

3. Westerhoff, ibid., p. 89. Italics in the original.

4. Ibid., pp. 89–99.

5. See John H. Westerhoff III and Gwen Kennedy Neville, *Generation to Generation: Conversations on Religious Education and Culture* (New York: The Pilgrim Press, 1974, 1979).

6. Westerhoff, *Will Our Children Have Faith?* op. cit., p. 100.

7. Ibid., p. 97.

8. As illustrated by his kind support of Thomas' struggle to believe, John 20:24–29.

9. As Peter discovers so movingly at breakfast by the sea, John 21.

10. Fowler calls faith at this stage "Individuative-Reflective" faith, comparable to Westerhoff's "Owned" faith, op. cit., ch. 19.

11. Steere's essay has recently become available again in *Gleanings, A Random Harvest: Selected Writings by Douglas V. Steere* (Nashville: The Upper Room, 1986). Rogers' essay appears as ch. 19 in his book *On Becoming a Person: A Therapist's View of Psychotherapy.* (Boston: Houghton Mifflin, 1961).

12. Rogers, op. cit., pp. 356–59.

13. For a complete discussion of these conflicts and the varied responses people make, see my *Frameworks: Patterns of Living and Believing Today* (New York: The Pilgrim Press, 1987), ch. 2.

14. Louis Dupres, "Spiritual Life in a Secular Age," in *Religion and America, Spiritual Life in a Secular Age,* ed. Mary Douglas and Steven Tipton (Boston: Beacon Press, 1982, 1983), p. 7.

Chapter 4 • Sharing Faith

1. See my *Frameworks: Patterns for Living and Believing Today* (New York: The Pilgrim Press, 1987), especially chs. 3 and 5.

2. I am indebted to Denham Grierson for this idea, although he speaks of "openings" in terms of identifying appropriate transformations to suggest to a congregation. See his *Transforming a People of God* (Melbourne: The Joint Board of Christian Education of Australia and New Zealand, 1984), especially ch. 3.

3. Walrath, op. cit.

4. Ibid., pp. 84–85.

5. See ibid., pp. 95–99.

6. Paul G. Johnson, "Making a Real Return to Church Possible," *The Christian Century* 104 (22):658, 1987.

7. Douglas Alan Walrath, *Leading Churches Through Change* (Nashville: Abingdon Press, 1979), ch. 3.

8. Available from the Alban Institute, 4125 Nebraska Avenue, Washington, DC 20016.

DATE DUE